EVERY STONE
A SERMON

Salt Lake Temple architectural rendering (1855) by William Ward from a design of Truman O. Angell, which hung in President Brigham Young's office for over twenty years.

EVERY STONE A SERMON

RICHARD NEITZEL HOLZAPFEL

BOOKCRAFT
Salt Lake City, Utah

Library of Congress Catalog Card Number: 92–70551

ISBN 0–88494–824–2

First Printing, 1992

Printed in the United States of America

For Jeni
22 April 1978
Salt Lake Temple,
and for our children,
Nathan, Zac, Zanna,
Marin, and Bailey

Contents

CONTENTS

Preface

Surrounded by a fifteen-foot wall, the Salt Lake Temple is located in downtown Salt Lake City, Utah, on a ten-acre parcel of land known as Temple Square, identified as the Temple Block or the Sacred Square during the nineteenth and early twentieth centuries. The temple, with its six spires rising from the east-central part of Temple Square, was envisioned by Brigham Young even before the Latter-day Saints arrived in the Great Salt Lake Valley in 1847.

The temple site was chosen only a few days following Brigham Young's arrival in the Great Basin on 24 July 1847. However, construction did not begin until the laying of the cornerstones on 6 April 1853. During the next four decades, work on the "Great Temple" was delayed many times, but beginning in the late 1880s, the Church's full resources were consecrated to the temple's completion—a temple that Church leaders consistently said fulfilled ancient prophecy: "And it shall come to pass in the last days, that the mountain of the Lord's house shall be established in the top of the mountains. . . . And many people shall go and say, Come ye, and let us go up to the mountain of the Lord, to the house of the God of Jacob." (Isaiah 2:2-3.)

"Come ye, and let us go up to the mountain of the Lord" reflects the imagery of not only the Latter-day Saints coming to Salt Lake City but also the many nonmembers who visited the site during its forty years of construction. This book contains "eyewitness" accounts of these people: their feelings, reactions, and experiences as they attended the temple cornerstone laying, capstone service, and dedication ceremonies. It is a centennial reminder of the Latter-day Saints' rich heritage.

This history is also a proper reminder of the devotion and sacrifice that went into the temple's erection, especially of those workers who were accidently killed during its construction—Archibald Bowman (1855); Sam Kaealoi (1878); William Pullen (1881); Samuel Ensign (1885); and Robert Ford (1890).[1] The temple stands in part as a monument to these laborers and to all who gave of their talents and physical means to erect it.

Brigham Young himself wanted the temple "to stand as a proud monument of the faith, perseverance and industry of the Saints of God in the mountains, in the nineteenth century."[2] The temple is a magnificent monument to their faith, but more important it remains as a sacred place of prayer, meditation, and worship.

While the year-by-year efforts to erect the Salt Lake Temple are outlined in this work, it is the sacrifices and the sense of holiness of these efforts which are highlighted. The cost to complete the Salt Lake Temple was estimated at just under three and a half million dollars when dedicated in 1893, but the cost in sacrifice on the part of the Saints, whether young or old, "will never be known until eternity shall reveal the secrets of this life."[3]

Acknowledgments

Many individuals encouraged and helped during the research and writing of this work, including Ronald Barney, George Bickerstaff, William Bollard, Scott Christensen, Greg Christofferson, T. Jeffery Cottle, Thomas Cottle, E. Lynn Dial, Randall Dixon, Jana Erickson, Steven Epperson, Garry Garff, Edward Griffith, Brian Hardy, Daniel Hogan, Jeni Holzapfel, Donald R. Jeffs, Edward Leo Lyman, Cory Maxwell, Veneese Nelson, Steven Olson, Melissa Ostler, Bruce Pearson, Billy Plunkett, Ronald Read, Ronald Romig, Dana Roper, R. Q. Shupe, William Slaughter, Steven Sorensen, Ted D. Stoddard, Linda Thatcher, George F. Tate, David Whittaker, and my students who attend the University of California, Irvine.

I have used the diaries, journals, reminiscences, and contemporary newspaper accounts of many who lived during the erection of the Salt Lake Temple. In doing so, where necessary I have spelled out abbreviated words and standardized spelling and punctuation to make the material more readable.

Several institutions have graciously provided copies of photographs and permission for their reproduction. I thank the Archives Division, Church Historical Department, The Church of Jesus Christ of Latter-day Saints, Salt Lake City, Utah; Photoarchives, Harold B. Lee Library, Brigham Young University, Provo, Utah; Visual Resources Library, The Church of Jesus Christ of Latter-day Saints, Salt Lake City, Utah; Photoarchives Department, J. Willard Marriott Library, University of Utah, Salt Lake City, Utah; the Museum of Church History and Art, The Church of Jesus Christ of Latter-day Saints, Salt Lake City, Utah; the Springville Museum of Art, Springville, Utah; the Utah State Historical Society, Salt Lake City, Utah; and the Small Prints Division, United States National Archives, Washington, D.C.

*The Kirtland Temple was the first temple erected by the
Saints and was dedicated in special services in 1836.*

1

"God Gathers Together His People in the Last Days"

The story of the Salt Lake Temple begins in Manchester, New York, in 1820 when a fourteen-year-old boy named Joseph Smith (1805–1844) prayed for guidance in the woods near his home. Joseph's religious quest ultimately brought a modern witness that God and Jesus Christ live—a new volume of scripture, the Book of Mormon, translated from an ancient record found near Joseph's home at the direction of an angelic personage named Moroni and published in March 1830. On 6 April 1830, the restored Church of Christ was founded, later known as The Church of Jesus Christ of Latter-day Saints.

During the next decade and a half, the Church grew dramatically but was subjected to legal and extralegal prosecution and persecution in New York, Ohio, Missouri, and Illinois. The Saints' unique beliefs and practices, coupled with the social intolerance common to the period, brought the Saints into direct and often bloody conflict with their neighbors.

Among the teachings characteristic of the restored Church was the doctrine of gathering. Gathering the Saints to specific geographical locations helped them concentrate their resources and energies to strengthen the Church and erect temples. Joseph explained, "God gathers together His people in the last days, to build unto the Lord a house . . . whereby He could reveal unto His people the ordinances of His house and the glories of His kingdom, and teach the people the way of salvation."[1]

Joseph Smith promised the Saints an "endowment of power" from God in the temples they built. Temple sites were designated in Ohio, Missouri, and Illinois. Despite the persecution they encountered, members of the Church felt a deep commitment to gather together, plan cities, and build temples.

The Saints believed that through good city organization and planning, they could provide for the wants—temporal and spiritual—of those who lived in the gathering places and ultimately create a perfect community. Joseph Smith's "Plat of Zion," a proposed city plan for the Mormon settlement in Jackson County, Missouri, was the guiding influence on the Saints' effort to build cities during the next fifty years.[2]

Joseph's plat of Zion called for the civic, governmental, social, and religious buildings of the community to be located in the very heart of the city. The city center was to be surrounded by homes and small businesses, with large tracts of land for agricultural use outside the city itself. The streets were laid out on a grid radiating out from the central temple complex.

Wide streets outlined blocks that were platted for individual family farms and businesses. Residences were spaced well apart from each other to provide open space and privacy. Specialized-use zoning, something original and novel for the period, separated residential, commercial, governmental, recreational, and agricultural use.

However, because of conflict between the Saints and their neighbors, only two temples, the Kirtland Temple in Ohio and the Nauvoo Temple in Illinois, were completed before the Saints' removal to the Great Basin in 1847. The Saints were able to worship in them for only a short period before they were forced to flee from their homes, farms, and temple.

The Saints began construction of the Kirtland Temple in 1833 and dedicated it on 27 March 1836.[3] The temple architecture is a blend of many styles and forms, including Federal, Georgian, Gothic, and Greek. The building incorporates many features and styles common to the period and to the Western Reserve area (northeastern Ohio) where it was built.

The Kirtland Temple, nevertheless, has several striking interior features that emphasize the unique uses of the building and that also distinguish the temple from other ecclesiastical buildings of the day. The first of these features is the two "courts" in upper and lower floors. The second is the pulpits found at both ends of the lower and upper assembly floors (the west-end pulpits being for the Melchizedek Priesthood, and the east-end ones for the Aaronic). The third is the use of curtains, or "veils," that were supported on rollers in the ceiling and could be lowered to create small classrooms and chambers.

A few years after the dedication of that first temple, following the removal of the Church from Ohio and Missouri, the Saints gathered on the banks of the Mississippi River to build Nauvoo—the City Beautiful. Joseph Smith's public announcement of the construction of the Nauvoo Temple on 3 October 1840 started the work that occupied the Saints until they left the city in 1846.[4]

In many respects, the Nauvoo Temple design was similar to the earlier Kirtland model, as both had a single bell tower and two major assembly floors that included raised pulpits, and finally an attic area with office accommodation mainly for priesthood leaders. Yet Joseph Smith's temple design in Nauvoo included several new innovations, such as a full basement reserved for a baptismal font used in the ordinance of proxy baptism for the dead. Baptism for the dead allowed worthy living Saints to be vicariously baptized for deceased friends or relatives. The temple in Nauvoo incorporated symbolic features into its exterior as well. The temple doctrine and theological significance of the Nauvoo Temple stand in marked contrast to the Kirtland Temple. In Kirtland, the temple endowment was an endowment of power; but in Nauvoo, the temple endowment was a richly symbolic series of ordinances and sacred ritual.[5]

When Joseph Smith and his brother Hyrum were murdered in Carthage, Illinois, on 27 June 1844, the Church's First Presidency—the chief presiding officers of the Church consisting of three members, a President and two counselors—was dissolved. The Quorum of the Twelve Apostles, the next administrative body in authority after the First Presidency, hastened to fulfill their martyred Prophet's vision and completed the Nauvoo Temple just before they were forced by mobs to abandon their city in 1846.[6]

The Saints sorrowfully left their newly completed temple at Nauvoo for the wilderness of Iowa, but they hoped that another temple could be built once they had located a place of refuge. While in Nauvoo, senior Apostle Brigham Young told a group of Saints, "We [will] go where we [can] be 'the old settlers,' and build larger Temples than this."[7]

Brigham Young led an advance company of pioneers to the Great Basin in 1847, while the majority of Saints remained at Winter Quarters (modern Omaha, Nebraska). Brigham arrived in the Salt Lake Valley on 24 July 1847. In recalling the event, Wilford Woodruff, an Apostle and later Church President, said President Young had seen the valley in vision earlier and now, still sick from a severe case of mountain fever, looked over the valley and said, "It is enough. This is the right place, drive on."[8]

Brigham Young and the Saints brought the city planning and temple building traditions of Joseph Smith with them to Utah. The Saints called this promised land Deseret—a term found in the Book of Mormon meaning honeybee and connoting industry and prosperity. Upon their arrival, the Saints applied for statehood but were given territorial status instead. Deseret was gradually reduced in size and was admitted into the Union in 1896 as the state of Utah.

The plat of the city of Zion and the architectural designs of both the Kirtland and Nauvoo temples played a significant role when Great Salt Lake City (later shortened to Salt Lake City), its temple, and the communities of the proposed state of Deseret were planned and designed.

Salt Lake City itself became the model for almost all Latter-day Saint settlements in the Rocky Mountains during the latter part of the nineteenth century. The social ideals of unity and order continued to knit the social fabric of Mormon life in Utah and in various Latter-day Saint settlements in the West. At the very center of Mormon society, the temple dominated the Saints' dreams and ultimately their practical considerations of community organization and structure.

Salt Lake City was organized around the Temple Block. Here Brigham Young declared to the faithful that the Saints would build another temple to their God. The Temple Block was not only the religious and social center of the community but also the geographical focal point of Deseret and its capital. At the southeast corner of Temple Square, surveyors established the Great Salt Lake "Base and Meridian." The survey point was used as the base reference point for survey work done in the region. Once identified, the Temple Block became a hub of Latter-day Saint activity in the valley.

*Brigham Young identified the site for the Salt Lake Temple
on 28 July 1847, just a few days following his arrival in the valley.*

2

"Here We Shall Build a Temple to Our God"

Orson Pratt and Erastus Snow, who had been sent ahead of the main pioneer company to scout a final approach to the valley, emerged from the mouth of a narrow canyon on 22 July 1847 and became the first Latter-day Saints to set foot upon their new land of promise. Upon viewing the Great Salt Lake Valley for the first time, both men instinctively shouted, "Hosanna! Hosanna! Hosanna!" and threw their hats into the sky. Elder Pratt later commented, "We could not refrain from a shout of joy which almost involuntarily escaped from our lips the moment this grand and lovely scenery was within our view."[1]

When Brigham Young entered the valley two days later on 24 July, the scouting party had already planted a prewinter crop and diverted the clear waters of City Creek for irrigation purposes. President Young and other Church authorities were pleased with what they found. Wilford Woodruff noted in his journal that it was "a land of promise, held in reserve by the hand of God for a resting place of the Saints."[2]

Only four days after Brigham Young completed the fifteen-hundred-mile trek to Salt Lake Valley, he walked to a spot between two creeks, waved his hand, and said, "Here is the forty acres for the Temple [later reduced to ten acres]."[3] His manuscript history states:

> This afternoon, accompanied by Elders Heber C. Kimball, Willard Richards, Orson Pratt, Wilford Woodruff, George A. Smith, Amasa Lyman, Ezra T. Benson and Thomas Bullock, I designated the site for the Temple block between the forks of City Creek, and on motion

of Orson Pratt it was unanimously voted that the Temple be built on the site designated.[4]

One of President Young's first acts in locating the temple site was to strike his cane forcibly on the ground and say, "Here we shall build a temple to our God."[5] Wilford Woodruff then drove a stake into the ground to mark the spot, which tradition indicates was located at the center of the finished temple. During the Church's April 1853 general conference, President Young recalled this experience:

> I scarcely ever say much about revelations, or visions, but suffice it to say, five years ago last July I was here, and saw in the Spirit the Temple not ten feet from where we have laid the Chief Corner Stone. I have not inquired what kind of a Temple we should build. Why? Because it was represented before me. I have never looked upon that ground, but the vision of it was there. I see it as plainly as if it was in reality before me. Wait until it is done. I will say, however, that it will have six towers.[6]

On 2 August 1847, Orson Pratt and Henry G. Sherwood began to survey the city and to lay it out into city blocks. They used the corner of the proposed Temple Block as a natural starting point, the Salt Lake Base and Meridian. A few days later, on 12 August, Orson Pratt and William Clayton determined the elevation of the Temple Block to be 4,309 feet above sea level. (Modern instruments have since determined the elevation at 4,323 feet above sea level.)

William Weeks, the Church's architect who helped build the Nauvoo Temple in Illinois, was among the Saints arriving in the Salt Lake Valley as part of the vanguard pioneer company.[7] Soon things seemed to be ready to begin planning for a new temple—the site was identified and the only person qualified in the Church to prepare working drawings of the temple was settled in the valley. President Young and a few members of the Twelve, assured that this was the right place for the gathering of the Saints and the location for the next temple, returned in August to Winter Quarters, where the other Apostles were preparing the Saints for next year's migration.

Formal meetings of the Quorum of the Twelve Apostles began again in earnest upon Brigham Young's return to Winter Quarters. By mid-November 1847, Church officials began to discuss the feasibility of reorganizing the First Presidency. Three weeks later, on 5 December, the Apostles present "unanimously elected [Brigham Young] President of the Church of Jesus Christ of Latter-day Saints, with authority to nominate . . . two counselors."[8]

On the following day, the new President called a council meeting at Brother Orson Hyde's house, where they "attended to several items of business [and] conversed about building a Temple in Salt Lake City."[9] Three weeks later, on 27 December, the new First Presidency was officially sustained by members of the Church in the area. For the first time since Joseph Smith's death in 1844, the Church was governed by a First Presidency and, under them, the Quorum of the Twelve Apostles.

In the meantime, unknown to President Young, several families in Salt Lake City, including William Weeks, decided to leave and return east during the following spring. Disappointed at the newfound Zion and discouraged by the painful experience of the exodus and the settlement in Utah, Weeks and those with him left both the Salt Lake Valley and the Church.

During Brigham Young's return trip, he encountered the group of disenchanted Saints heading east from Salt Lake City. Both camps were located at Ash Hollow on opposite sides of the river some three hundred and eighty miles from Winter Quarters. When President Young talked with

them, he discovered that Weeks, according to Thomas Bullock's account, "had run away from Ash Hollow two days ago. He was afraid to see Brigham." Brigham in turn told the camp leaders to tell Weeks, "We can build a Temple without his assistance, altho' he says we cannot."[10]

While William Weeks's departure may have initially dampened the prophet's hopes in preparing the architectural drawings of the proposed temple, other more pressing concerns occupied his attention when he arrived in the valley shortly thereafter. From the time President Young identified the temple site until early 1853, not much planning or effort went into erecting the building. The Saints were preoccupied with settling and establishing their new homes in the wilderness. Forts were built, fields prepared, homes constructed, life sustained, and countless other tasks were performed to prepare for the mass emigration of the Latter-day Saints still to come. These first years were difficult, but the Saints' desire to build a temple was not diminished.

The first move toward beginning the temple was the creation of the Public Works Department on 26 January 1850 located on the Temple Block. Daniel H. Wells was appointed to act as the superintendent; on 26 May 1850, Truman O. Angell was appointed public works architect and eventually Church architect, replacing William Weeks.[11] Angell served in this position until his death in 1887. While acting as Church architect, Angell wrote, "I labored as hard as any man could."[12] Sometime later, in contrast to William Weeks's self-importance, Angell reflected, "I feel a good deal worn out, but if the President and my brethren feel to sustain a poor worm of the dust like me to be Architect of the Church, let me strive to serve them and not disgrace myself. This I trust and mean shall be my aim. May the Lord help me so to do."[13]

Within a year of Angell's assignment, the Church voted officially to support President Young's desire to build a temple in Salt Lake City. During the Church's April 1851 general conference, just four years after the pioneers' arrival in the valley, the Saints sustained by acclamation the motion to erect the temple. Daniel H. Wells was appointed as a committee of one to supervise its building, along with the Public Works Department.[14]

Under Wells's direction, public works crews began to build public and church buildings, roads, water systems, and other projects that could not be carried out by private individuals. Projects built by public works laborers included the Council House, the Social Hall, the Church Historian's Office, a public bath house, the General Tithing Office, the Bishop's Storehouse, the Salt Lake Theater, a "Spanish" wall around the city, and an official residence for the newly appointed territorial governor, Brigham Young. Beginning in 1852, Daniel H. Wells's crews also worked at the temple site, where they built a wall around the Temple Block.

As work progressed on private homes and other public buildings in the valley, President Young told the Saints that "by the help of the Lord and this people" he would build a house to the Lord in Salt Lake. He then added: "Will he dwell in it? He may do just as he pleases; it is not my prerogative to dictate to the Lord. But we will build him a house, that, if he pleases to pay us a visit, he may have a place to dwell in, or if he should send any of his servants, we may have suitable accom-modations for them." President Young reasoned, "I have built myself a house, and most of you have done the same, and now, shall we not build the Lord a house?"[15]

The work of preparing the architectural drawings for the "House of the Lord" and supervising much of the work at the temple site fell upon Truman Angell. Although he gladly accepted this assignment, Angell found the transition from a carpenter who had earned his living by working with his hands to one who spent his time using his mind a difficult and frustrating one. "It is a trifle to labor with one's own hands [in comparison] to the labor of the mind," he wrote. "While one tires the extremities," he noted, "the other wearies the man in his whole system."[16]

Angell helped Brigham Young and other Church officers officially start the forty-year construction effort by participating in the cornerstone-laying ceremonies on 6 April 1853. Angell himself assisted the First Presidency in laying the southwest cornerstone.

*The ground breaking and site dedication ceremony for the temple
was held on 14 February 1853.*

3

"Beneath the Reach of Mountain Floods"

The ground breaking and site dedication of the Salt Lake Temple occurred on Valentine's Day, 14 February 1853, in preparation for the laying of the temple's cornerstones during April general conference. It is difficult to imagine the scene, even though a photographer present captured the momentous day through the medium of a daguerreotype. Salt Lake City at the time was still a small frontier community. The first pioneer company arrived in the valley just five and half years earlier, and each following summer new emigrants arrived with few provisions and possessions. The pioneer economy was still very fragile when the ground was broken for this enormous construction effort, projected to cost millions of dollars.

An anonymous Saint left his recollection of the event and the economic situation of many of those attending:

> I walked [to the meeting] the morning the ground was broken for the foundation of the Temple . . . on the Temple Block. I went through frozen mud and slush with my feet tied up in rags. I had on a pair of pants made out of my wife's skirt—a thin Scotch plaid; also a thin calico shirt and a straw hat. These were all the clothes I had. It was go that way or stay at home. . . . I was not alone in poverty. . . . There were many who were fixed as badly as I was.[1]

A prominent participant, Wilford Woodruff, wrote the following in his journal on 14 February:

> This was an important and interesting day to the Saints in the Valley and even in all the world. The Saints met upon the Temple Block in a vast body to break the ground for another Temple. The people commenced gathering at an early hour and at eleven o'clock there were thousands upon the ground.[2]

"President Young arrived at half-past ten, with his councilors in the First Presidency, Heber C. Kimball and Willard Richards," wrote John D. T. McAllister, a participant in the events.[3] The First Presidency and those assembled then "witnessed the survey of the site of the Temple, by Jesse W. Fox, under the superintendence of Truman O. Angell, Architect."[4] This activity took about half an hour. At eleven o'clock in the morning, the services began.

The Church leaders and fellow Saints then moved to the east line of the survey, and Marshall Jesse C. Little, assisted by the police, identified the various lines to the assembly, who had formed a hollow square around the lines. They remained in this position while the President, along with the First Presidency, got into a "buggy inside the square surrounded by the Quorum of the Twelve."[5] Brigham Young then arose and addressed the people assembled "in a most thrilling speech of about thirty minutes, so as to be heard distinctly in all parts of the vast assembly."[6]

President Young briefly recounted the trials and persecutions the Saints had endured in Ohio, Missouri, and Illinois before the Lord led them to the "consecrated spot." He told recent converts not to "be discouraged because they had not had all the privileges that many of the older members had, of being robbed, and driven and mobbed and plundered of everything they had on earth, for he would promise all who would remain faithful" that they too would be tried in all things.[7] He then said, "We shall now again attempt to build another Temple. We have tried it many times [before]. We may not now, but we will try it."[8]

Heber C. Kimball then offered the prayer of dedication. He "arose and with uplifted hands to Heaven offered up a fervent heartfelt prayer to God imploring his blessing upon President Young, Counselors, and all the authorities of the Church [and] the whole house of Israel."[9] He also dedicated the ground "unto God and prayed for the blessings of the Lord to attend them in building the Temple."[10] At the close of the prayer, the Church's presiding officers moved to the southeast corner of the ground laid out for the temple.

John D. T. McAllister described the scene at the site by saying, "There was from one to three inches of snow on the ground, but it was a clear and lovely day. The sun soon scattered the snow, and in some places the ground was left quite bare; with some six inches of frost in the earth."[11] In his account of the proceedings Wilford Woodruff also noted the wintry conditions at the site:

The ground being frozen, President Heber C. Kimball commenced breaking the ground with a pick. . . . Then the ground was broke and President Young took out the first turf. . . . While taking it out [a] silver dollar was flung from someone in the congregation which struck in the hole. Brother Kimball said that was an omen that we should have plenty of money to build the Temple.[12]

President Young commented that "it was his privilege to remove that, and took the lump about one foot square upon his spade, and lifted it high up, and said 'get out of my way, for I am going to throw this.' And there he held it about one minute, before he could get room to lay it down, from off the temple site, so dense were the multitudes around."[13] He then closed the meeting by declaring the ground broken for the Great Temple and blessing the Saints, to which all assembled responded, "Amen!"[14]

When the meeting ended, the congregation "rushed forward to the hole to get a chance to throw a little dirt out." Wilford Woodruff, his father, who was seventy-eight years of age, and Wilford's twelve-year-old son "all flung out dirt of the foundation for this important temple."[15] Some "one hundred and fifty laborers, I should judge continued the work," wrote Lorenzo Brown.[16]

The feeling of many present was expressed best by one participant when he said, "I should like to live long enough to see such a stupendous work completed, and wished that I might be there to see the cap stone laid with a shout, and to receive the favors and blessings of God in the structure."[17] Only a few of those present, however, would witness the capstone-laying ceremonies thirty-nine years later.

On 21 February 1853, President Young assigned Elder Wilford Woodruff the task of preparing the foundation for the laying of the cornerstones during the upcoming April general conference. Elder Woodruff arrived at the temple site on the following day and "found it a busy place" as he began his effort to dig the foundation with the other men.[18] Wilford, who had endured the persecution in Ohio, Missouri, and Illinois, wrote in his journal as he began his new assignment, "May the Lord enable us to finish it."[19] During a particularly busy week, he simply noted, "March 14, 15, 16, 17, 18, and 19th I spent this week in digging out the foundation for the Temple."[20]

The workers diligently continued their task—even the day following a severe snowstorm on 24 March—to have things ready for the cornerstone-laying service on 6 April.[21] The only breaks were Sundays, 27 March and 3 April; otherwise, work continued unabated. As Elder Woodruff noted, "I spent my time at hard labor to prepare the Temple ground for laying the corner stones of the temple."[22]

During the ground-breaking services, President Young promised the Saints, "In a few days I shall be able to give a plan, at least on paper."[23] In fulfillment of this promise, President Young visited Truman Angell and drew on a slate the outlines of the temple he had seen in vision several years earlier. William Ward, Angell's able assistant, recorded:

Brigham Young drew upon a slate in the architect's office a sketch, and said to Truman O. Angell: "There will be three towers on the east, representing the President and his two counselors; also three similar towers on the west representing the Presiding Bishop and his two counselors; the towers on the east the Melchizedek priesthood, those on the west the Aaronic priesthood. The center towers will be higher than those on the sides and the west towers a little lower than those on the east end. The body of the building will be between these and pillars will be necessary to support the floors."[24]

On 17 March 1853 Truman noted, "I find my journal neglected. I shall proceed to bring it up to date. My time has been since the 12 February spent mostly on the design of the Temple . . . and laying out the foundation of the Temple."[25]

A written description of the proposed temple appeared a year and a half later in the Church's newspaper, the *Deseret News,* on 17 August 1854. This article became the basis for non-Mormon newspaper articles about the Saints' effort to build the Great Temple during the following decade. The *Illustrated London News* published an article in 1857 entitled, "Mormon Temple in Salt Lake," containing many specifications of construction based on the Angell article, including a large woodcut illustration of the temple.[26]

Although the main elements of the temple were based on President Young's vision, the design of the details and the styles of the building seem to come from Angell himself. Ward recalled, "On several occasions the foundation and thickness of the walls was the subject of conversations. But I do not recollect any talk between Brigham and Angell in regard to the style of the building. Angell's idea and aim was to make it different from any other known building, and I think he succeeded as to the general combination."[27]

The anticipated day soon arrived for the cornerstone laying. Members of the Church from far and wide gathered at the Temple Block. Many Church officers and missionaries had been called home from their assignments to participate. Elder Lorenzo Snow, of the Quorum of the Twelve

Apostles, recalled, "[I] had been called home from [my] European mission in order to be present. . . . [I] waived an intended voyage around the world and arrived here in time."[28]

The *Deseret News* noted, "Wednesday, April 6, 1853, could not have dawned a more lovely day, or have been more satisfactory to Saints or Angels." The editorial continued, "The distant valleys sent forth their inhabitants, this valley swarmed forth its thousands, and the most glorious sight has not been seen for generations than at Great Salt Lake City this day."[29]

One participant at the services noted: "The sun, the sky, the atmosphere, the earth appeared neither too cold nor too hot nor lukewarm; all seemed filled with life; adapted to each soul, to cheer and make happy every individual of the many thousands of aged, middle-aged and youth, who had assembled from the near and remote parts of the inhabited valley."[30]

The crowd gathered at the old Tabernacle with three bands, military companies, a choir, and Church leaders. The company then moved eastward across the Temple Block with the "National Flag unfurled from its top most staff, the ensigns of the various bands and escorts floating in the breeze, and the banner of 'Zion's Workmen' towering aloft" as they proceeded to the southeast corner of the temple grounds.[31] "The crowd was so great it was very difficult to see and hear," Lorenzo Brown noted. "However, [I] got where I could see those on the north side."[32] The cornerstone-laying ceremony began after the congregation found its place.

The First Presidency—Brigham Young, Heber C. Kimball, and Willard Richards—along with Patriarch John Smith laid the first cornerstone. A hymn was sung by the choir, which included the following stanza:

> Deep in this holy ground
> These corner stones are laid.
> Rejoicing thousands round,
> O God! implore thine aid:—
> That Zion now may prosper'd be,
> And rear a Temple unto thee.

President Young then stood upon the stone and spoke:

Wilford Woodruff journal entry for 6 April 1853.
Note the drawing of four cornerstones in upper left.

This morning we have assembled on one of the most solemn, interesting, joyful, and glorious occasions, that ever has, or will transpire among the children of men, while the earth continues in its present organization, and is occupied for its present purpose; and I congratulate my brethren and sisters that it is our unspeakable privilege to stand here, this day, and minister before the Lord, on an occasion which has caused the tongues and pens of prophets to speak and write for many scores of centuries which are past.[33]

He continued: "But what are we here for this day? To celebrate the birthday of our religion! To lay the foundation of a Temple to the Most High God, so that when His Son, our Elder Brother, shall again appear, he may have a place where he can lay his head, and not only spend a night or a day, but find a place of peace, that he may stay till he can say, I am satisfied."[34]

President Young then concluded his remarks by saying: "We dedicate this, the South-East Corner Stone of this Temple to the Most High God. May it remain in peace till it has done its work, and until He who has inspired our hearts to fulfill the prophecies of his holy prophets, that the House of the Lord should be reared in the *'Tops of the Mountains,'* shall be satisfied."[35]

Heber C. Kimball dedicated the stone, beginning in this way: "O God the Eternal Father, in the name of thy son Jesus Christ of Nazareth, we ask thee to look upon us at this time in thy tender mercy. Thou beholdest that thy servants Brigham and his council, have laid the Chief Corner Stone of the holy House, which we are about to erect unto thy name. We desire to do it with clean hands and pure hearts before thee, and before thine holy angels."[36]

Following the choir's rendering of a hymn entitled "The Temple," written by Eliza R. Snow, the procession moved to the southwest corner. The southwest cornerstone was laid by the Church's Presiding Bishopric. Presiding Bishop Edward Hunter addressed the congregation and was followed by his counselor Alfred Cordon, who offered the prayer of dedication. The choir then sang a specially written song for the occasion, entitled "The Corner Stone."

The congregation moved to the northwest corner of the temple site to witness that cornerstone laid by the presidency of the high priests quorum, the stake presidency, and members of the stake high council. John Young then spoke, after which Elder George B. Wallace offered the consecrating prayer. The choir sang, "Come Saints of Latter Days."

The northeast cornerstone was laid by the Quorum of the Twelve, the Presidency of the Seventies, and elders quorums. Parley P. Pratt, a member of the Quorum of the Twelve, then gave a Spirit-filled address to the people. He reminded the Saints:

And again the Lord has ordained that all the most holy things pertaining to the salvation of the dead; and all the most holy conversation and correspondence with God, angels and spirits shall be had only in the sanctuary of his holy Temple on the earth; when prepared for that purpose by his saints; and shall be received and administered, by those who are ordained and sealed unto this power; to hold the keys of the sacred oracles of God.[37]

Interpreting the words of Isaiah and Micah as found in the Bible, Elder Pratt continued:

To this same principle the prophets Isaiah and Micah bear testimony, saying, "that in the last days all nations shall go up to the house (or temple) of the Lord, in order to be taught in his ways and to walk in his paths, for out of Zion shall go forth the law" etc. . . . Ye Latter Day Saints! Ye thousands of the hosts of Israel! Ye are assembled here today and have laid these Corner Stones for the express purpose that the living might hear from the dead; and that we may prepare a holy sanctuary where *"the people may seek unto their God; for the living to hear from the dead,"* and that heaven, and earth, and the world of spirits, may commune together.[38]

He promised the Saints that through the completion of the temple, "the kings, nobles, presidents, rulers, judges, priests, councilors, and senators which compose the general assembly of the church of the first born in all these different spheres of temporal and spiritual existence, may sit in grand council" on the earth, to concert measures for the overthrow of tyrants—both religious and political—sin, and death. He concluded:

Saints! These victories will be achieved, and Jesus Christ and his saints [will] subdue all opposing powers, . . . as sure as innocent blood was ever shed on mount Calvary, or the official seal broken on the door of the tomb of the

Son of God. This day a work, in laying these Corner Stones for a temple, amid the mountains, is one advancing step in the progress of the necessary preparations for these mighty [changes]. . . .

But remember, O ye saints of the Most High!—*remember*, that the enemy is on the alert. That old serpent and his angels, who have ruled this lower world with few exceptions, for so many ages, will not tamely and without a struggle, submit, to have the kingdom, and seat of government, and sanctuary of our God again erected on our planet. . . . No! From the moment the ground was broken for this Temple, those inspired by him have commenced to rage; and he will continue to stir up his servants to anger against that which is good; but if we are faithful, the victory is ours, in the name of Jesus Christ: AMEN.[39]

Elder Orson Hyde then offered the dedication prayer for this stone. He prayed, "Although thou are exalted in temples not made with hands in the midst of the redeemed and sanctified ones,—yet deign thou to meet with us in our humble sphere; and as we have laid, help thou us to dedicate unto thee this Corner Stone of Zion's early Temple, that in her courts thy sons and daughters may rejoice to meet their Lord."[40]

The choir sang "Proclaim to All People We've Laid the Foundation of a Temple," and then Brigham Young ascended the northeast cornerstone and blessed the Saints:

Brethren and Sisters, I bless you in the name of Jesus Christ of Nazareth, and pray my Father in Heaven to encircle you in the arms of his love and mercy; protect us until we have finished this Temple, and receive the fulness of our endowments therein, and then build many more; and I pray also, that we may live to see the great Temple in Jackson County, Missouri. You are now dismissed with the blessing of the Lord Jesus Christ upon your heads, Amen.[41]

"The corner stones now rest," the Presidency wrote in their ninth general epistle, "in their several positions, about sixteen feet below the surface of the eastern bank, beneath the reach of mountain floods" and "so deep beneath the surface that it will cost robbers and mobs too much labor to raze it to its foundation."[42] Brigham Young said at a meeting held later in the day, "This day, and the work we have performed on it, will long be remembered by this people, and be sounded as with a trumpet's voice throughout the world. . . . It is a day in which all the faithful will rejoice in all time to come."[43]

On the following day, Elder Parley P. Pratt told the Saints attending the general conference that he had had an unusual experience at the laying of the cornerstone the day before. "Shall I speak my feelings, that I had on yesterday?" he asked the congregation. "Yes, I will utter them, if I can. It was not with my eyes, not with the power of actual vision, but by my intellect, by the natural faculties inherent in man, by the exercise of my reason, upon known principles, or by the power of the Spirit, that it appeared to me that Joseph Smith, and his associate spirits, the Latter-day Saints, hovered above us on the brink of that foundation, and with them all the angels and spirits from the other world, that might be permitted, or that were not too busy elsewhere."[44]

A witness to the proceedings, Joseph Curtis, noted in his diary, "[April] 6th. I witnessed the laying [of] the corner stones of the temple. O Lord may I never forget . . . listening to the remarks of the servants of God."[45] The First Presidency agreed, "The Holy Spirit has been in our midst, and the revelations of Jesus have guided His Apostles and Prophets, in laying the Corner Stones of the Temple, and ministering unto the Saints, during Conference, in an unusual degree, which has caused much gladness of heart, and great joy and rejoicing."[46]

In their annual message to the Saints throughout the world, printed just a few days later, Church leaders called upon the Saints to bring "your silver, your gold, and everything that will beautify and ennoble Zion, and establish the House of the Lord." Never forgetting the reality of pioneer life, they added, "Not forgetting the *seeds* of all choice *trees, and fruits, and grains, and useful productions* of the *earth,* and labor-saving machinery, keeping yourselves unspotted from the world by the way side."[47]

*Salt Lake City in 1853. The Temple Block is located in
the upper right with uncompleted wall surrounding the site.*

Long after the events of this period, Saints recalled fondly their participation in the beginnings of the Great Temple. The efforts of Edward Simons of Bountiful, Utah, in this undertaking were remembered in his obituary in 1895. "He was one of the first workmen on the foundation of the Salt Lake Temple," his wife, Jane, noted with a deep sense of honor.[48] It was a glorious thing for the Saints to participate in any position in the erection and construction of the Great Temple. They remembered that participation all their lives and were honored for it at their deaths.

By June 1855, a sixteen-foot-deep, red-sandstone foundation was finished. The sandstone was quarried from Red Butte Canyon northeast of the city. It was here that the first accident occurred that took the life of a workman. On 12 January 1855 at 2:30 P.M., twenty-seven-year-old Archibald Bowman was killed when "a large quantity of earth and rock" fell on him. His obituary noted, "He died as he had lived, doing good, being

crushed when warning another of the danger." Bowman lingered just a few hours before he succumbed to his injuries.[49]

While several hundred men worked on the structure and others brought lumber from Big Cottonwood Canyon, work at the temple site continued intermittently, depending upon the fragile pioneer economy and the previous year's harvest.

In 1856, during one of the periods of food shortages in the Salt Lake Valley, Charles Rockwood noted: "After the bran was all consumed we were three weeks without bread, meat or milk. [We] only had to sustain life from what could be gathered as greens from the fields consisting principally of cat tails, roots, thistles, pigweeds and other greens."[50] In spite of these difficulties, the Saints continued their efforts to build the noble edifice in the desert as they established a community in the Salt Lake Valley. On several occasions, however, work stopped completely.

The stonemasons at work at the temple site,
Tabernacle and Endowment House in background.

4

"Every Stone in It Is a Sermon"

The story of the building of the Salt Lake Temple is one of great sacrifice, dedication, and commitment. Several years following its completion, Elder J. Golden Kimball said:

> When I think about [the temple], every stone in it is a sermon to me. It tells of suffering, it tells of sacrifice, it preaches—every rock in it, preaches a discourse. When it was dedicated, it seemed to me that it was the greatest sermon that has ever been preached since the Sermon on the Mount. . . . Every window, every steeple, everything about the Temple speaks of the things of God, and gives evidence of the faith of the people who built it.[1]

The progress of the work on the Salt Lake Temple was often tied to events unforeseen by the Saints. The first major interruption occurred in 1856 when Truman Angell was sent on a mission to England to study various architectural styles in an effort to make Brigham Young's vision a reality.

Angell had been working on the temple plans through January 1856, but these efforts had left him exhausted and somewhat depressed. His poor health and his fragile economic condition, along with the lack of progress on the temple, caused Angell to weary of his task. President Young thought it wise to send him on a working vacation—an architectural mission to Europe.

The work did not completely stop; however, it was significantly curtailed by Angell's absence. He noted in his journal on 3 April 1856, "I was asked by President Brigham Young at his table to visit Europe." The prophet told him:

> You shall have power and means to go from place to place, from country to country, and view the various specimens of architecture that you may desire to see and you will wonder at the works of the Ancients and marvel to see what they have done: and you will be quick to comprehend the architectural designs of men in various ages. . . . Take drafts of valuable works of architecture, and be better qualified to continue your work and you will increase in knowledge upon the Temple and other buildings, and many will wonder at the knowledge you possess.[2]

President Young himself had been in England as the leader of the Council of the Twelve's mission to Great Britain several years before (1840-41). While there, Elders Young, Kimball, and Woodruff spent twelve days together in London visiting the sights, among which were some of the great architectural monuments of England. He wanted Angell to have the same experience, which he hoped would help inspire Angell as it had done him.

After three weeks of preparation, Truman Angell left Salt Lake City on 13 July 1856. His assistant, William Ward, was left in charge of the building project.

While in England, Angell had an engraving of the temple design, based on a daguerreotype of the rendering, prepared by a recent Mormon convert, Frederick Piercy. During his mission, Angell traveled extensively throughout Great Britain and visited the continent. He preached the gospel on numerous occasions and visited many important architectural monuments.

wall be no more obstacle than a thread paper. This wall was one of Brigham's *ruses* to keep the people constantly employed, and accustom them to the idea of having to *defend themselves* at some future day.

We enter at the north gate of this city wall, climb an elevation to our left, and Salt Lake City lies before us. It is a small city spread over a large surface. It has about 15,000 inhabitants, and covers an area of six square miles. Of these 15,000 inhabitants, at least 10,000 are females. A large proportion of the men in this city are polygamists; almost all the "authorities of Zion" live here with families comprising from *twenty-five* to *two* wives each, and there are many more girls than boys born. This proportion is increased by many married men being absent on missions; and would be still larger were it not for the number of single young men who are compelled to be bachelors from the scarcity of single females. This population is perfectly heterogeneous; at least two-thirds are English and Scotch people. Welsh, Danes, and Americans compose the remaining third part. I think that certainly not over one-sixth of the inhabitants of Salt Lake City are Americans; and they are generally from the Western frontiers, with the narrow prejudices and ignorance common to their birth-place.

The city is divided into square blocks containing ten acres each, and intersected at right angles by streets one hundred and thirty-two feet wide. At the edges of the sidewalks flow little streams of cold, clear water. These are conducted over all the city; they are obtained from several of the many mountain creeks that pour down their melted snows into the Salt Lake. Their water is used for irrigating the soil, without which neither spring flowers, early vegetables, nor cereals could be cultivated. Along the margins of these streams—which materially help to enhance the beauty of the place, as well as increase the comfort of the inhabitants—are planted many cotton-wood, locust, and other rapidly-growing trees. Their green liveries give the city a very charming relief, in contrast with the desert and desolate valley. From our point of view (*vide* engraving), Heber C. Kimball's block of buildings are to our right. To our right, a little below, is the Temple block, surrounded by a wall and trees. Parallel with this is the Tithing Office—here are deposited the contributions of the faithful. On a line with this are the buildings of Brigham Young.

Let us pay Brother Brigham a visit. It is about four o'clock in the afternoon, and Brigham is most

NEW TEMPLE TO BE BUILT AT SALT LAKE CITY.

the workmen obtain their flour and provisions. We observe a group of women, with generally common and pale faces, who are waiting for their "men's pay," which they have to almost beg from the surly fellow who attends to them. These small houses we pass next are the mansions in which D. W. Wells's wives reside. They are almost mud hovels. Mr. Wells is a "prophet, seer, and revelator," as well as second counselor to Brigham. He has some six ladies in his sanctified harem; two of them are sisters, and *report* says they often manage to get up any thing but the heavenly scenes befitting such a paradise begun. We next come to Brigham's orchard. He is a

COUNCIL HOUSE, SALT LAKE CITY.

probably at his office, and will receive us affably. We pass the Tithing Office; notice that it is a large *adobé* building, with several offices attached, where

great lover of fruit, and has a great family who are great lovers of fruit too. They, however, are carefully excluded from the orchard; peach-trees

THE TABERNACLE.

and apple-trees would soon be desolate else. Here is the "Lion House." This is a long house, with the first story in stone. In front, on the top of this first story, is a very well sculptured lion, with his head dropped on to his stretched paw. This is intended to represent Brigham Young—"quiet but watchful." In this house some seventeen or eighteen of the prophet's wives reside. Brigham used to have them scattered over different parts of the city, in houses of all sorts of sizes and styles. He says, however, *and of course no one would have suspected such a thing if the prophet had not said so,* "he could not trust them out of his sight," and so he had to put them all together. We will get Brigham to allow us the privilege of peeping at them presently; for, although a second sultan, he does not command his ladies to *veil* in

MORMON THEATRE.

the presence of strangers. If he be in a good-humor with the party, he seems rather proud of the long row of good-looking faces.

We remark the pointed gable and little peaked garrets on the "Lion House," and pass on. We walk by three little neat offices, and then stand in front of Brigham Young's mansion. This is a handsome two-story edifice, built of *adobé*, nicely plastered and dazzlingly white. It is balconied from foundations to roof. On the top is an observatory, whence Brigham can overlook the dreary city and the dull valley, and sometimes take a peep at the stars, whose bright eyes seem to dance with mirth as they quiz Salt Lake and its doings. The whole is surmounted by an imitation bee-hive, which is intended as the symbol of Utah.

We open the gate, walk up the steps, when the door opens, and face to face, on his own door-sill, we confront the famous prophet Brigham Young.

In person he is above the medium height and a little inclined to corpulency. He is dressed in black cloth, and, although the air is very warm, he is well wrapped up in an overcoat. His habits of life make him very sensitive to the slightest change in the atmosphere. He has suffered a good deal in his younger days, and with this the cares of his family—for his children are very refractory—begin to weigh heavily upon him. His constant struggles and difficulties with the United States officers not only try his patience, but also wear his body. His consuming anxiety about his object of ambition—the establishment of an independent kingdom—and his efforts to maintain the people in constant and implicit submission, are sufficient to leave their mark on any man's physique. He is now fifty-six years old; and, although young-looking in features, still evinces his age in person. His face is indicative of penetration and firmness. Some ladies think him very handsome; but his lower lip, if nothing else, eminently betrays the sensual voluptuary. To strangers he is very courteous, but easily offended by any slighting allusion to the people or their polygamy.

"Good-evening, Mr. Young. Will you permit us to inspect your mansion?"

"Certainly, gentlemen; and, as I have a spare hour, I will chaperon you myself."

Blessing our stars for our good fortune, we follow our host into his drawing-room. There sits a good-natured lady, "fat, fair," and *fifty*. She is Brigham's senior wife, and is called Lady Young. There sits another person, about thirty, who smiles very sweetly at Brigham on his entrance. She is very good-looking, tall and majestic in figure, oval

features, soft blue eyes, light brown hair, and wearing an expression of subdued intelligence. She is Brigham's favorite wife; that is, he shows

SALT LAKE CITY, UTAH TERRITORY.

While in France, Truman received word that he should return to Utah as soon as possible. William Ward had quit his position and had left Utah, leaving the work unsupervised. Angell was ready to return to his work, determined to complete a building suitable to its purpose. He arrived home on 29 May 1857 after traveling 16,569 miles, according to his estimate, during his thirteen-month mission. He immediately began preparing detailed drawings for the temple so that stones could be quarried and brought to the temple site for placement in the walls.

Only a part of this work was completed when the one hundred thousand subscribers of the popular magazine *Harper's Weekly* got a firsthand account of the "City of the Saints." The long article contained several illustrations. The principle illustration, however, was the architectural rendering of the proposed "New Temple to Be Built at Salt Lake City." The article stated:

It covers an area of ten acres, and is surrounded by an *adobe* wall, with a neat stone coping, around which are trees. We enter the block at the east gate. Right before us are the foundations of the Mormon Temple. This is already—though not quite level with the ground—quite a stupendous undertaking. . . . Its entrance will front the east, with a massive gateway. Its foundations, which are foolishly costly, are of solid rock. They are sixteen feet deep, and as much wide. With the wall surrounding the block, they have already cost $1,000,000 in labor and materials. . . . They have now resolved to erect it entirely of cut stone. Its plans are publicly exhibited, and, should it ever be completed, it will form a very magnificent pile. Its architecture will be original, and is meant to be allegorical.[3]

A month following the appearance of the *Harper's Weekly* article, Brigham Young asked Wilford Woodruff to gather Church leaders at the temple site for another important event, the placing of historical items in the record stone in the temple foundation. President Young's journal entry for 13 August 1857 states in part, "At 6:30 p.m. [I] met with Elder [Heber C.] Kimball,

[Daniel H.] Wells, [John] Taylor, [Willard] Richards, [Wilford] Woodruff and several others . . . to deposit the records of the Church, in the south east corner of the temple wall."[4] Elder Woodruff noted that he and President Young "packed the books in a stone box two and a half feet long, twenty inches deep, and one foot seven inches wide. It was filled with our works." At 7:45 P.M., the "lid was put on, soldered with lead and covered with plaster [of] paris and turned bottom side up and set in the south east corner."[5]

The contents of the special box included several Book of Mormon foreign language editions; a copy of the Doctrine and Covenants; Church newspapers and pamphlets; portraits of Church leaders; and several denominations of gold coins minted in Salt Lake City.

A prayer of dedication was given by President Young, in which he asked:

O God our Eternal Father, we ask thee in the name of Jesus Christ that thou will bless this deposit which we have made in the foundation of this temple. We dedicate all these books, papers, records and history unto thee O Lord our God. And I pray in the name of Jesus Christ, Our Father in Heaven that thou wilt preserve this deposit . . . that it may endure that no mildew or decay may come upon it until it shall come forth for the benefit of the House of Israel and thy people that it may be a benefit unto them. . . . Preserve these records as thou didst the pot of manna hid up by Aaron that they may be preserved to come forth in the own due time of the Lord. All these blessings we ask in the name of Jesus Christ Amen.[6]

During his prayer, President Young made several references to the impending event that would ultimately stop work on the temple during the next several years—the coming of the United States Army to Utah.

This second major interruption in the temple construction resulted from federal officers grossly misunderstanding and misrepresenting Church leaders' intentions in the new territory. Under the command of Colonel Albert Sidney Johnston,

United States president James Buchanan sent an army of some twenty-five hundred soldiers to Utah to quell a reported rebellion against federally appointed territorial officers.

The fact that President Buchanan did not inform Brigham Young, acting governor of the territory, of the expedition's mission increased the fears of the Saints about the government's intentions. When news arrived in Utah of the approaching army, Church authorities and local government leaders decided to resist, perceiving the army to be nothing more than an organized mob like those the Saints had encountered in Missouri several years earlier.

It was rumored that General William Harney, the original leader of the military expedition, intended to capture and execute Brigham Young and then winter the army on the Temple Block in the uncompleted temple.

Negotiations between Church leaders and federal representatives finally ended the crisis, but while Johnston prepared to march his troops through Salt Lake City to a point southwest of the city, Brigham Young planned a drastic step to prevent the plunder and occupation of the Mormon settlements, particularly Salt Lake City, if the army did not keep its pledge to march through the city and establish a camp away from any Latter-day Saint settlement.

A representative of the army, Captain Stewart Van Vliet, was invited to attend a Church service in the Old Tabernacle and learned firsthand what the Saints planned to do in such an event. George A. Smith reviewed the preparation made by the Saints to defend themselves and stated that the people "are willing any moment to touch fire to their homes, and hide themselves in the mountains, and to defend their country to the very last extremity" if the army did not abide the conditions of the settlement.[7]

The evacuation, known as the "move south," began in late March and lasted nearly two months, which put virtually the whole of northern Utah's population, nearly thirty thousand people, on the road and in temporary settlements in Utah Valley, south of Salt Lake Valley. A few men left behind were ready to set Salt Lake City ablaze if the army attempted to occupy the city.

Among those who fled south was Truman Angell, who had boxed up all the temple drawings and instruments. Some of the boxes were taken south, while others were hidden in Salt Lake City. The Saints also took actions to prevent the army from desecrating the temple site itself.

Brigham Young had dirt hauled to the Temple Block to cover the foundation so the area would resemble a freshly plowed field before the army arrived. Another group of public works laborers hid all of the cut stone for the temple in an effort to prevent detection of their activity by the invading army.

Captain Albert Tracy, a commanding officer of a component of Johnston's army, noted in his diary on 26 June 1858:

We entered Emigration Canyon. . . . Opening out from the last rough gorge, we entered upon a broad plateau, or bench, and Salt Lake City lay at our feet. We are surprised and refreshed with its general appearance of neatness and order. The buildings were almost entirely of adobe, giving them the appearance of grey cut stone. They were set well apart, nearly each by itself, and within the enclosures about them one saw that which one so longs to see from long familiarity with these deserts—perfectly bright green and luxuriant trees and shrubbery.[8]

Tracy then noted, "And now came a spectacle not common." The city was completely deserted. "It was substantially a city of the dead," he wrote. "The rich strains of our Band, then were wasted somewhat except to our own ears, upon these echoing, empty streets and tenements."[9] The army passed through Salt Lake City across the Jordan River to establish a new military post several miles from Salt Lake in Cedar Valley, as they had promised to do.

The Saints returned to their homes, workshops, and temple site beginning in July 1858. For the next three years, however, work on the temple was at a virtual standstill as an uneasy peace existed between federal troops and the Church members.

Brigham Young announced to other Church leaders in December 1859 that "we must commence [the work on the temple] next spring [and] uncover the foundation." Brigham already knew, before the foundation was uncovered, that the rubble overlying the foundation proper and immediately under the flagstone layers seemed to have less stability than required. "I shall have to take up one tier of rock all over the foundation," he said at the meeting.[10] Eventually, the temple area was cleaned to expose the original sandstone foundation.

Once the dirt was removed from the area and the flagging and rubble were removed from the foundation, stone of the best quality could be substituted and work on the actual construction could be continued with renewed energy. Granite was eventually chosen for the main structure, thus ensuring the realization of President Young's vision of a temple that would stand beyond his own generation. He said in 1863, "I want to see the Temple built in a manner that it will endure through the Millennium."[11] The granite chosen for the temple walls was much more substantial material than the adobe or sandstone that had previously been discussed, and came from the stone quarries at Little Cottonwood Canyon some twenty miles southeast of Salt Lake City.

The small quarry at Little Cottonwood Canyon operated intermittently from 1860 to 1870 under the direction of John C. Livingston. Livingston was sent to the quarry to establish a permanent operation in a little hollow at the mouth of the canyon on the north side of the creek, following the completion of the transcontinental railroad. He supervised the work there until the temple was completed in 1893, even though he had lost his right hand and arm in an accident during the construction of the railroad.

Granite City, the name of this thriving little community, had as many as fifty buildings—mostly stores, boardinghouses, and cabins. Many of those who lived there worked as miners and teamsters for the mines farther up the canyon. The Latter-day Saint quarrymen lived in a small encampment of

Foundations of temple, Old and New Tabernacles.

21

A settlement at Little Cottonwood Canyon was established to support the Church's quarry where the granite stone was obtained for the temple.

tents pitched around the cook house, and the Church teamsters lived around the cattle pens.

Sometime during the spring of 1874, the quarrymen moved to another site where they had found a better quality of stone, about one and one-half miles farther into the canyon. This site became known as Wasatch. Utah photographer Charles Carter visited the site in 1875 and noted in his record: "It is best to show where the rock is quarried which is at the mouth of Little Cottonwood. The rock is cut roughly in large squares preparatory to its transit to the Temple Block. All the rock had to be brought by teams which was very arduous work as the wagons were constantly breaking down and squares of granite had to be left by the roadside."[12]

The first stones, weighing from twenty-five hundred to fifty-six hundred pounds, were brought to the temple site by teams and wagons from the quarry. The workers often took as many as four days to haul one huge block from the quarry to the Temple Block. Annie Wells Cannon remembered "the sight of the great stones one at a time being hauled along the streets by two yoke of oxen and we would all stand for them to pass with a feeling of awe and reverence."[13]

The small stones were hauled on wagons, but the larger stones were hung under them. Many of the wagons broke down during the immense effort to transport the stones, and the road to Salt Lake was often littered with old wagons during the summer seasons. Joseph Fielding Smith, a young man at the time and later Church President, recalled:

In the summer much of my time was spent in Little Cottonwood Canyon, and there I watched the men digging and blasting the great granite blocks and preparing them for delivery to the temple. I can remember the days of the ox teams and how they tugged with their heavy loads, and how at intervals down the canyon road rough-cut blocks had skidded from the wagons and were lost.[14]

While some laborers at the quarry were supported through the Public Works Department or donations, other workers supplied their own housing and donated their time. John Nielsen recalled: "I contributed one dollar each month for a long time toward paying the men who were working in the Temple Square, cutting rock for the walls of the Temple. I also worked some in the rock quarry up in the mouth of Little Cottonwood Canyon. While doing this I boarded myself, furnished my own bedding, and donated my work."[15]

While many stonecutters worked in the canyon at the quarry, others continued their work at the temple site in Salt Lake City.

The Temple Block was a favorite playground for children who lived near it, and games of hide-and-seek among the huge stones and the foundation were a favorite. Young James Henry Moyle's family lived nearby—his father was a stonecutter from England and worked at the site where young James played.

As he grew to manhood, James Moyle learned his father's trade. He recalled the work at the temple site, where he labored under his father:

Not only days, but weeks, were required to dress some of the stones, and high wages, as much sometimes as one hundred dollars each, were paid for preparing a single stone. . . . The stone steps in the Temple with a nose on them brought the worker about seventy-five dollars each. Making the nose was delicate work. Many stones in the building required a high degree of skill on the part of the worker, for these come almost to a feather edge. One may see them from the ground in the large round windows. The grain is easily cracked since the small pieces of quartz, feldspar and mica in the composition fall apart when jarred. For this reason the feather edge was always cut last. If there was a miss-hit, or if a given blow of the hammer were too hard, the work went for nothing, and weeks might be lost.[16]

A group of workers known as the Dinner Bucket Club met at the Knox Carpenter Shop on the Temple Block during the lunch hour to discuss the day's affairs. Sometimes they focused on local and regional politics, and at other times they turned to the news from foreign lands; but they always viewed their discussions through the lens of the Church that had brought these men together from all over Europe and North America.

Young James Moyle, though not a member of the club at first, sat in Brother Knox's shop during lunchtime to listen to the discussions, and this stimulated the young man's interest in learning. Moyle worked at the temple site, before and after a mission, to help pay for his education at a local university. Upon returning from his mission, Moyle's work on the temple resumed on 28 November 1881. "Had a rock brought into the shed yesterday," he wrote in his journal. He attended various Church meetings, wrote a history of his missionary experience, and "worked on rock" during the next few days.[17]

When he had saved sufficient funds, Moyle began to correspond with several law schools, including Harvard. Eventually, he left the trade of his father and grandfather and headed east to attend the University of Michigan, where he successfully completed a law degree.

Tithing collected locally and shared from general Church funds employed carpenters, stonemasons, sawyers, and other skilled artisans. These men received their wages in tithing scrip, goods, and at certain periods in cash. Moyle received a pig for payment on one occasion; he sold it for almost thirty-three dollars.

Since the workers relied on tithing donations for most of their pay, the work at the Temple Block varied from just a few men working during economic hard times to hundreds when the local economy was better.

Another stonecutter, Benjamin T. Mitchell, arrived in Utah on 5 August 1855. "Soon after I arrived [in Utah] I went to work at stone cutting for Brigham Young," he recalled, "and in a few days was put as foreman over the Stone Shop at the Public Works [Temple Block] and continued my labors as such and was appointed Bishop over the 15th Ward about the first of January 1857."[18] Mitchell worked in his professional and ecclesiastical duties until the "move south" in 1858. Following the Saints' return to Salt Lake City, he was released as bishop but "continued in charge of the stone cutting on the temple until April 1864," when he started cutting stone for the city.[19]

When the new city hall building was completed, Mitchell returned to work on the temple. Within a short time, however, he was working on another building in Salt Lake City, a local bank in 1866. When the bank building was finished, he went back to the temple to continue cutting stone with his sons, except when "building for myself and jobbing occasionally for others as opportunity permitted." Eventually, most laborers at the Temple Block were called away for another project—completing the transcontinental rail lines approaching the territory. Mitchell noted:

[I] went and worked on the railroad cutting stone until completed and then went back to work on [the] temple again with my boys and continued until the fall of 1874. [I] then sent two of my boys to cut stone on the St. George Temple continuing [to work] on the temple myself until the spring of 1875 when myself and two boys [were] called to work on the big Co-op Building all the time being dictated by the Council of the First Presidency.[20]

The work on the new Zion's Co-operative Mercantile Institution (ZCMI) building provided necessary cash payments to Mitchell and his sons. He wrote, "While laboring on the temple for two years without cash or store pay [I] became destitute of clothing and provision for my family."[21]

Even during difficult times there was usually some activity going on at the temple site. Workers could always expect visits from interested persons—members and nonmembers of the Church—who found themselves in Salt Lake City for various reasons.

Visitors arrived almost daily at the Temple Block, including recently arrived immigrants. Because the donations for the temple project were collected from every member of the Church, no matter where they lived, Latter-day Saints everywhere were interested in its progress. Often the temple site was one of the first places to visit following their arrival in the valley.

Elder B. H. Roberts recalled his arrival in Salt Lake City as a ten-year-old boy from his native home in England in 1866. As Captain Chipman's ox team company turned onto Main Street, he "found himself at the head of the lead yoke in that team." The Saints "turned out to welcome the plains-worn emigrants and were standing on the street sides to greet them."[22] At the head of Main Street, the immigrants took their wagons into the Church stock corrals:

The cattle were soon freed from the yoke and seemed delighted with the straw and hay brought them. Across the way on Temple Square block, the foundations of the temple rose above the general level of the surrounding ground and seemed to be an object of interest to nearly all the emigrants, many of whom were permitted to go within the wall, and view it.[23]

Another immigrant related the importance attached to the Temple Block by the newly arrived immigrants when he recalled, "While in Old World, [I] read an account in the Deseret News of [the laying of the cornerstones of the temple in 1853], that grand, joyful, yet solemn occasion. . . . A year later, [I] gathered [to] Zion, [seeing] the Temple . . . next to seeing the Prophet, [was] the uppermost ambition of the soul."[24]

James A. Garfield, future United States president, arrived in Salt Lake City on 11 August 1872 just before eight o'clock in the evening. On the following day, Elder George Q. Cannon "took us in a carriage to the various points of interest in the city," Garfield noted in his diary, including "the Tabernacle [and] the Temple."[25] Over the years the Temple Block attracted other notable figures.

United States presidents Ulysses S. Grant and Rutherford B. Hayes; Sir Robert Burton, world-renowned English explorer; the youthful Samuel Clemens, later known as Mark Twain; Artemus Ward, American humorist; Baron Lionel de Rothschild, European financier; Ralph Waldo Emerson, essayist and poet; Dom Pedro, emperor of Brazil; Horace Greeley, editor of the New York *Tribune;* Henry Ward Beecher, Protestant preacher; Henry Stanley, explorer of Africa; and Joseph Smith III, the martyred LDS prophet's son, all visited the Temple Block and witnessed the progress of the temple's erection.

Theodor Kirchhoff, a German traveler, visited the city in 1867. "At the north end of the street I saw to the left a high fieldstone wall and about it, a large roof that resembled the back of a giant turtle," he wrote. The roof of course was the "world-famous Mormon Tabernacle." He continued:

I went unhindered through an open gate to a construction site, to get a better look at the strange building. One of the workers, a Norwegian whom I met at the little overseer's shack by the gate, offered to be my guide. With thanks I accepted this friendly offer. Near us on the spacious grounds was the foundation for tomorrow's grand Mormon Temple. Huge blocks of hewn granite, here in profusion, clearly proved Mormon earnestness about erecting the magnificent church that I saw in blueprint in the overseer's shack. . . . Still, whether the Mormons would be able to finish such a massive work seemed to me very problematical.[26]

When Ulysses S. Grant and his wife arrived in Utah in early October 1875, "carriages were in waiting for us; . . . the street was lined with rows of children, I should say three deep," Julia Grant recalled.[27]

Several derricks were built at the temple site to assist in placing the temple wall stones on the building.

Eventually four large derricks were used at the temple site to swing the stones into place after the workers had hooked the stones onto winch lines.

A steam engine was brought to the temple site to power a derrick sometime in 1876, and following the completion of the Logan Temple in 1884, a second engine was brought to Salt Lake and used to lift stones at the temple site.

Several thousand Sunday School children greeted the presidential party as they left the depot and traveled on South Temple Street to the Temple Block. The children were "all singing songs of welcome and literally strewing the President's roadway with flowers," Mrs. Grant added.[28]

During the procession, President Grant asked Utah governor George W. Emery whose children they were, as he had heard so many negative comments about life in Utah that he could not believe such well-dressed and behaved children could come from Latter-day Saint homes. "Mormon children," Emery replied. The president hesitated for several moments and "murmured, in a tone of self-reproach, 'I have been deceived.' "[29]

The president's wife recalled her visit to the temple site:

Our visit here was most interesting. I went with two of the elders . . . to the Temple. These gentlemen conducted me through [the] great [Tabernacle], had the magnificent organ play for me, and, as the great volume of solemn sacred music filled the [Tabernacle], I could not help kneeling with bowed head and my heart, always so susceptible to the power of music, full of tenderness, to ask God's blessing to these people. The gentlemen asked if I had offered a prayer for them. "Yes," I answered, "a good Methodist one."[30]

Joseph Smith III visited Utah as the president of the Reorganized Church of Jesus Christ of Latter Day Saints, headquartered at Lamoni, Iowa. He wrote about his first visit to the Mormon capital in late fall of 1876 in his organization's newspaper, the *Saints' Herald*: "We visited the temple grounds, where work was just closing up for the winter season. The walls are now twenty or more feet above the water table, and seem in a fair way of going up. . . . We inscribed our names in the visitors' book in which we saw the names of General U. S. Grant, General W. T. Sherman, Dom Pedro, and other of similar, and less, note."[31]

Four years later, Utah territorial governor Eli H. Murray invited Rutherford B. Hayes to visit Utah during a presidential tour of the western United States. "I am glad to know of your pro-

posed [visit] to the west and write now in advance," Murray wrote, "to express the hope that you will stop, take a look at this great Territory and dwell for a while within the gates of the City of the Saints." The governor argued, "Salt Lake City is a good halfway place, a sojourn here would prove both refreshing and interesting."[32]

President Hayes accepted the governor's invitation and, with his wife and several other members of the presidential party, arrived in Utah on 6 September 1880. While the president did not make entries in his personal diary during this trip, a Washington newspaper, the *National Republican*, reported the president's movements daily while he was gone from the nation's capital.

First Presidency members John Taylor and George Q. Cannon, along with several other "leading Mormons, including some ladies who gave a bouquet to Mrs. Hayes," met the president's train in Ogden. On the following day, 7 September, the presidential party left the Walker Hotel in Salt Lake City early and "rode about the city returning to the hotel at ten o'clock."[33]

While the presidential visits by Hayes in 1880 and Harrison in 1891 were not as intimate as Grant's visit had been several years earlier, their visits demonstrate the interest Utah engendered in people. In most cases, the Temple Block was one of the first sites in Salt Lake City visited by the curious, the interested, and the devout. Those who visited the site often received pieces of temple granite as souvenirs.

Grant Brothers Stages brought visitors to the Temple Block to see and explore the temple site.

Sometimes there was much laughter at the site. An elderly gentleman recalled such an incident at the Temple Block: "A Swede drove [one of the carts]. When a rock was chained to the cart, he would sort of chirp to them [the oxen], then whistle, and finally say, 'Ve is ready, Yonny an' Yake. Move along an' take anudder rock for the House of the Lord.' "34

"Yonny" and "Yake" did not move much and paid very little attention. President Young and Bishop Joseph Sharp were watching, and soon Bishop Sharp took the whip and asked the Swede if he could take over. Having spoken to the oxen, which were his own, three times, he "whirled the bull whip around his head and brought it down across the backs of both oxen." The oxen went right through their ox staples "as though they were matches." It took the workers nearly an "hour to get them back." All the time President Young did not say a word but "went away holding his sides and laughing."35

There were times when laughter was not heard at the temple site, however. On 27 September 1878 Sam Kaealoi, a native of the Marquesas Islands (one of the French islands in the South Pacific), was accidently killed when he fell some thirty-five feet from the scaffolding on the temple, fracturing his skull. A doctor at the site "attended immediately, but gave no hope of his recovery, and the unfortunate man died a few minutes afterwards." Brother Kaealoi had arrived from his homeland to Zion only a few months before "and had been employed as a workman on the Temple from that time till his death," a newspaper reported.36

Labor on the temple slowed at the end of the 1868 season when work on the transcontinental railroad, which was now approaching Utah Territory, took most of the materials and human laborers. The brief sacrifice of manpower to assist in completing the railroad system ultimately aided in the completion of the temple itself by replacing the ox teams with the train system.

A track running up South Temple Street into the Temple Block from the city station was completed in 1873. Simultaneously, a railroad side line was completed to the stone quarries in Little Cottonwood at Wasatch, where an abundant amount of high-quality granite was found within one mile of the little town. During the first year of its existence, Wasatch listed some thirteen individuals as official residents. By 1883, it had grown to over three hundred people. By 13 September 1873, a derrick was built at the temple site in Salt Lake City to assist in placing stones for the temple walls. Eventually, four large derricks were used at the temple site.

Sometime in 1876, a steam engine was brought to the temple site to power one derrick. Brigham Young noted in August 1876 that a large group of men were working on the temple "who have been sent by the various quorums of the priesthood and sustained by them during their labors. They are doing a good work." More important, though, "for the first time in the history of building temples to the Lord," Brigham continued, "so far as I am acquainted, we are now laying the rock by the help of the steam engine, and the speed and ease with which it does its work is very encouraging."37

During the April 1876 general conference, the "people in mass [were] called upon to rise up and build the Temple."38 Several weeks later, Church officers were sent by President Young to the outlying communities and settlements in an effort to emphasize the conference message. On 22 May 1876, Elders John Taylor, Wilford Woodruff, and Franklin D. Richards traveled to Ogden by train to make such an attempt. Elder Woodruff recorded, "I went to Ogden today with Elder John Taylor and several other Elders and Bishops to attend a priesthood meeting in the Tabernacle for the purpose of assisting to make arrangements for continuing the building of the Temple in Salt Lake City."39

This effort was followed by a First Presidency circular, *To the Bishops, Seventies, High Priests and Elders,* under the signatures of John W. Young and Daniel H. Wells "of the First Presidency" and John Taylor "in behalf of the Twelve Apostles," issued sometime during the fall of 1876. The circular reemphasized an earlier statement by Church leaders "that the labor upon the Temple here [Salt Lake City] will continue to be pushed forward by those now engaged in it."40

Church leaders called upon the priesthood quorums to continue their efforts on the temple and in the quarry so "that the work upon the Temple may progress as fast as practicable, during the winter, and that preparations may be made for the accomplishment of a good work the next summer." While the need for "competent workmen to do the fine cutting" was strongly emphasized, more important was the need of priesthood quorums to "provide for the payment" of these highly skilled men.[41]

The revival of the united order during the 1870s gave Brigham Young hope that both the temple in Salt Lake City and the other temple under construction in St. George could be completed earlier than he expected.[42] In a letter dated 26 October 1874, President Young noted with some degree of hope, "The temple is looming up fine and we may expect the rock work to be pushed another season as it has never been. Our increased facility for laying rock and the prospect of working into the United Order bid fair to complete both temples at an early date."[43]

Following special services in 1877 in the temple at St. George where Church leaders dedicated parts of the building, Brigham Young returned to Salt Lake City. On his way home, he stopped at Manti, a settlement one hundred and twenty miles south of Salt Lake City, and dedicated a site for another small temple. Within three weeks, he had done the same in Cache Valley, eighty miles north of Salt Lake City, at Logan, Utah.

The emphasis on temple construction in other Mormon settlements also increased efforts to complete the temple in Salt Lake City. President Young wrote in May 1877, just three months before his death:

The present year is one that thus far has been unparalleled in the history of The Church of Jesus Christ of Latter-day Saints. . . . Within a period of less than six months, one Temple has been completed and dedicated, and the site for two others consecrated to the Lord our God

Orson Pratt made his astronomical drawings of the moon phases based on his observations at the Salt Lake Observatory (bottom right) in 1878.

and the work of construction commenced thereon, whilst another (the one in this City) is being pushed forward with greater zeal and energy than has before been manifested since its commencement.[44]

Within two years of Brigham Young's death, the Salt Lake Temple walls were about forty-five feet in height. The work of the 1879 season included the laying of the fifty symbolic moon stones depicting the 1878 lunar cycle.

The responsibility to provide the necessary astronomical information for the proper depiction of the fifty moon stones fell upon Orson Pratt. Elder Pratt established an adobe astronomical observatory on the southeast corner of the Temple Block in 1869, known as the Salt Lake Observatory, one of a series of observatories erected from Cambridge, Massachusetts, to San Francisco, California, under the direction of the United States Coastal Survey.

Two full transits of the night sky could be observed through Elder Pratt's English telescope's three-inch lens when the row of wooden slats in the observatory roof was opened. The primary purpose of the observatory was to obtain meridian-solar readings every day at noon to ascertain the correct time for the community's clocks and watches. However, in 1878, Elder Pratt spent a significant amount of time plotting the lunar cycle for the year in preparation for the laying of the fifty symbolic moon stones. Of interest is the fact that on the east central facade, the moon is depicted in its four phases during the month of April, a significant month for Latter-day Saints, since it was the time of the Church's organization in 1830 and the season of Easter.[45]

Orson Pratt died in his home several years later on the morning of 3 October 1881, the same day "a melancholy accident occurred on the Temple now in course of erection in this city," the *Deseret Evening News* published.[46] Sometime between one and two o'clock in the afternoon, William Pullen fell from the wall into the uncompleted basement. It seems that a sudden gust of wind against a derrick pulled a rope he was holding, and as a result he lost his balance and fell some sixty feet. "The poor fellow was carried into a house on the Temple Block, and was immediately attended to by Doctor Richards," the news story continued. Pullen died at 3:30 P.M. from internal injuries.

Sometime the same year, John Starley, an English convert to the Church, took a position as a "night watchman" at the Temple Block. Later, the Presiding Bishop of the Church, William Preston, asked him, "Brother Starley, I understand you were trained in gardening and landscaping. How would you like to take over the job of making the 'Temple Block' into a beautiful garden?" John Starley had received training as a young man from his father, who had been in charge of the vicarage farms and gardens of Bolney and the Church of St. Mary Magdalene in Brighton, England.

Brother Starley accepted the position and immediately went to work. According to his history, the west part of the Temple Block was "planted with lawns and gardens. The east half was being used by masons and builders of the Temple and was not put into lawns and flower beds until the Temple was completed." John spent several weeks in the nearby canyons to obtain suitable trees to plant at the Temple Block.[47]

Another fatal accident occurred at the temple site during this period. Samuel Ensign, an eighty-year-old English convert who had worked at the temple from the time the foundation was laid until he was too old to continue such physical labor, remained at the construction site as a sort of caretaker ensuring each evening that everything was in proper shape after the work crews left. Joseph Smith III, who was visiting Salt Lake at the time, recalled:

He loved the work of the Temple so much he would not consent to stay away from the building, insisting that he might be allowed to do something. On this day [24 June 1885], in walking across an open well where a stairway would ultimately be built, he slipped on the planking loosely laid over the opening, fell a distance of ninety feet and was instantly killed. I attended his funeral held in the Assembly Hall, a building which stands on the Temple lot, one of the most artistic edifices in the city. The speakers on the occasion were Nicholson, Groo, Kesler, and Sheets, who paid glowing tributes to the character of the sturdy old man.[48]

A few months later, in late October 1885, the *Deseret Evening News* reported that the "work of rock laying on the Temple, in this city, this season, has been confined to the east end until today, when, the towers being squared up, the workmen reported to the west towers and commenced operation there."[49]

Work on the Salt Lake Temple slowed again during the particularly frustrating period of Utah history known as the Federal Raid.[50] United States marshals and their deputies "raided" the homes, businesses and public buildings in the Latter-day Saint communities throughout the western United States in an attempt to arrest polygamous members of the Church, especially Church leaders, for violation of anti-polygamy laws. As a result, many Church members and leaders were forced to go

"underground" to avoid arrest; despite their efforts, however, many were found and arrested.

The government's prosecution of individual Church members was soon enlarged to include the corporate body of the Church. This action culminated as federal officials attempted to enforce the Edmunds (1882) and the Edmunds-Tucker (1887) acts.

These acts officially dissolved The Church of Jesus Christ of Latter-day Saints as a legal corporation, disfranchised Utah women, abolished the territorial militia, and disfranchised and provided for imprisonment of those practicing plural marriage. It also allowed the government to control public schools and escheat all Church property with a value of fifty thousand dollars or more that was not used exclusively for religious worship.

Government officers set out immediately to confiscate Church holdings in the territory in an effort to force the Saints to comply with federal

Salt Lake Temple construction workers:
1) W. Chapman, 2) W. Knox, 3) J. Dover, 4) J. Moyle, 5) T. Jones, 6) W. McGregor, 7) D. Thomas,
8) P. Gillespie, 9) J. Howells, 10) J. Morgan, 11) J. Oppenshaw.

law—a law the Saints considered a violation of the First Amendment, which guarantees freedom of religion.

Frank H. Dyer, like the Northern carpetbaggers who arrived in the South following the Civil War, came west hoping to capitalize on the federal appointments in Utah Territory. He was eventually appointed the receiver of Church property. Dyer entered a suit to obtain the Temple Block, but the Church was able to regain control of the property after arguing that the Temple Block was used exclusively for religious purposes and therefore was not subject to confiscation. The territorial supreme court, however, left an opening for future action when it said that any property that helped to support illegal activity—in this case, teaching or encouraging the practice of polygamy—could be confiscated.

While the federal government's intervention caused untold sacrifices for families whose fathers were imprisoned or in exile, one of the greatest challenges the Church faced during this period was the inability to acquire and hold the necessary funds to complete the Salt Lake Temple, along with its many other obligations, including providing for the needs of the poor. President John Taylor died in exile in July 1887; and Wilford Woodruff, the senior member of the Quorum of the Twelve, became the leader of the Church during this particularly difficult period.

Salt Lake Temple under construction, ca. 1891.

5

"I Want to See the . . . Temple Finished"

President Woodruff's first public appearance following the death of President John Taylor was a long-awaited moment for the Saints who had had little contact with Church leaders during the intense period of persecution and prosecution.

Lorenzo Snow and Franklin D. Richards accompanied him to the Tabernacle on the Temple Block just before the beginning of the Church's general conference in the fall of 1887. The white-haired leader was immediately greeted with warm applause, which did not subside until he arose from his seat and waved to the multitude. President Woodruff noted in his personal journal that evening, "I, for the first time in about three years, went into the great Tabernacle and met with 10,000 Saints and spoke to them [for] thirty minutes."[1] No attempt was made to arrest him, but since it was unwise to remain so visible in Salt Lake City, President Woodruff left before the closing hymn.

While underground, President Woodruff met with other General Authorities to discuss Church affairs, including the work on the temple. A question concerning a change in the temple spires was presented to Truman O. Angell. Shortly after responding to these and other changes on the temple plans, Truman died in Salt Lake City on 16 October 1887. Daniel H. Wells, for years Angell's supervisor at the Temple Block, said in tribute to his dedication, "As long as the Salt Lake Temple stands, that is monument enough for him."[2]

Joseph Don Carlos Young, son of Brigham Young, succeeded Angell as the Church's architect, a position he served in until 1893. As the chief Church architect during the final years of the construction of the Salt Lake Temple, Young contributed significantly to the temple's final form, including the proposed changes approved by Presidents John Taylor and Wilford Woodruff.

On 3 December 1888, President Woodruff met with seven of the Twelve Apostles and the Presiding Bishopric. Of that meeting he wrote, "It was decided that the Presiding Council of the Church should direct the building of the Temple and the [Presiding] Bishopric should collect the means and the Architect should draw the plans and visit the temple and see that the building was erected according to the plans."[3]

Several months later, the First Presidency was reorganized, and Wilford Woodruff was sustained as the fourth President of the Church. Eventually, with the resolution of political and legal problems between the federal government and the Church, a new phase of work on the temple began under the direction of Wilford Woodruff.

Wilford Woodruff was sustained as the President of The Church of Jesus Christ of Latter-day Saints on 7 April 1889 at the Church's general conference. Within the month, President Woodruff's journal indicates increased activity on Salt Lake Temple matters, including a visit to the Little Cottonwood quarry on Independence Day for a celebration:

We went to Wasatch, a settlement of our people in the Little Cottonwood Canyon where our brethren are splitting our granite rock for [the] Salt Lake Temple. It was an immense affair. Granite rocks seventy feet square split up into building blocks. The brethren had

Oxen for the Salt Lake Temple baptismal font.

formed quite a settlement of tents and lumber houses and very fine flower gardens. [They] had streams of water in small troughs running all through their settlement. The creek abounded with trout. We had a good dinner, speeches, music, and dancing. We returned [to Salt Lake City] at 8 o'clock. Distance of the day fifty miles. We had a very pleasant time. About two hundred people attended. One peculiar feature in the place was all the rattle snakes were on the north side of the creek. None in the settlement.[4]

At the conclusion of the construction season in 1889, the temple stood a little over one hundred sixty feet above ground. President Woodruff's diaries during the period suggest his interest in completing the temple as soon as possible and his personal involvement with almost every decision. In May 1890, he met with the Church architect and the Presiding Bishopric to discuss the budget for temple construction for the next working period— "$50,000.00 . . . for the work on the Temple this season."[5] During the next few months, final decisions on heating, electrical power, and other physical-facility matters were made.

During this period of increased concern about completing the temple, the Church continued to feel the effects of the Edmunds-Tucker Act of 1887. In an effort to curb Mormon immigration to Utah, the federal government dissolved the Perpetual Emigration Fund Company. This organiza-

tion was the Church's chief agency for immigration. Nearly twelve thousand members of the Church lost their voting rights, including Utah's female population, and no Latter-day Saint immigrant was considered worthy of becoming a United States citizen or of having the right to vote.

The most significant threat to the completion of the temple occurred during the summer of 1890. Democrat Frank Dyer, receiver of Church property, was criticized by Republican officials for allowing a compromise between Church and government attorneys that enabled the Temple Block and the other Utah temples to remain in Church hands. Dyer was eventually replaced by Henry W. Lawrence, an ex-Mormon and former temple ordinance worker and bishop. The United States attorney for Utah, C. S. Varian, moved against the Temple Block property and the other temples at St. George, Manti, and Logan, Utah. Varian argued that these properties did not meet the criteria established by the territorial supreme court for exemption from confiscation by the government, since he claimed that Latter-day Saint teachings encouraged polygamy and the temples were used by the Church for preaching.

As Church authorities sought to address the political and economic problems that confronted the Church, the desire to complete the temple in Salt Lake City became a prime focus of President Woodruff's efforts. He wrote in his journal that after much anguish, prayer, and discussion with his counselors, he was prepared to act "for the temporal salvation of the Church."[6]

On 24 September 1890 President Woodruff issued the Manifesto, which stated that the Church was no longer teaching plural marriage nor permitting anyone to enter into it. He expressed his intent to obey the laws of the land, even though he believed those laws to be unconsitutional since they infringed on the Saints' freedom of religion. Nevertheless, President Woodruff believed that only by abandoning plural marriage could the Saints retain use of the three completed Utah temples in St. George, Logan, and Manti and have the freedom and necessary resources to complete and then dedicate the Great Temple at Salt Lake City. It took some time for the government to respond to the gesture offered by President Woodruff.

The visit of United States president Benjamin Harrison in Salt Lake City in May 1891 exemplifies the efforts of federally appointed officials to continue to alienate the Saints. These officials prevented the president from visiting the most important and well-known tourist site in the territory, the Temple Block, by scheduling other "official" activities in the city.

As had become the tradition during a presidential visit, the Sunday School children lined the street to welcome the official party to Utah. As the procession moved along South Temple Street, the group "encountered a surprise of a most inspiring character." Some six or eight thousand children "neatly attired, and each [having] a United States flag," stood in line waiting for the nation's president. The children greeted President Harrison with "three tremendous cheers, which fairly rent the air." The newspaper account continued, "The procession stopped and the President stood, hat in hand, while the children sang, 'My Country 'tis of Thee' and 'The Star Spangled Banner.' They kept time by waving the flags."[7]

President and Mrs. Harrison were deeply moved by the display and moved on to their hotel. The children walked to the Temple Block and joined the Tabernacle Choir in a rehearsal in preparation for the presidential visit to the Tabernacle.

The children had "prepared to render patriotic music" for the presidential party, accompanied by the famous organ and choir. To the children's great disappointment, they were dismissed when Church officials received word that the president was not coming. Mrs. Harrison, however, did arrive shortly thereafter and "expressed her disappointment" when she learned that the children had planned a special concert for her and her husband.[8]

Such public displays of patriotic support were an important part of the Church's efforts to let Washington officials know of their sincerity in making an attempt to reconcile with the government, while still maintaining their core beliefs. The Manifesto was also part of this important process and an important step toward gaining the economic and political freedom the Saints had been denied for so long. It was hoped that these efforts would also allow the Saints to retain the use of their temples and the Temple Block.

On 7 October 1891 during a priesthood leadership meeting held in the Salt Lake Eighteenth Ward chapel, President Woodruff said, "I never would have issued the Manifesto had it not been for the inspiration of God to me. I want to see the Salt Lake Temple finished and [as] poor as I am, I will donate $500.00 towards this work. The Lord also wants it completed, and I ask you brethren to try and collect enough for this purpose."[9] Church leaders now turned their attention to concerns other than political persecution, such as the completion of the Salt Lake Temple. Work progressed rapidly until the walls of the building were finished. Regrettably, one last fatality at the temple site occurred at this time. Robert Henry Ford, an immigrant from England, died at the Deseret Hospital in Salt Lake City on 23 January 1890 from the effects of a fall from the temple wall earlier.[10] The work on the exterior walls was completed, and full attention was focused on the interior.

In an effort to obtain the necessary skilled laborers to complete the interior work on the temple, some missionaries were called home from their fields of labor. Elder Abraham H. Cannon of the Quorum of the Twelve Apostles attended a meeting with Presidents Wilford Woodruff and Joseph F. Smith of the First Presidency and Francis M. Lyman of the Quorum of the Twelve to discuss several business items, and "it was decided to release Brother Dahlquist from the Swedish mission." The missionary was called home "to do necessary carving work in the Temple of this city."[11]

Also, in 1890 Church leaders decided to move forward in calling several Latter-day Saints who had shown artistic promise on "art missions" to Paris, France.[12] John Hafen, Lorus Pratt, and John B. Fairbanks were set apart for their special art mission on 3 June 1890 by Elders Heber J. Grant, Anthon H. Lund, and Seymour B. Young. Within twenty days, the three art missionaries left Utah for Paris.

John Fairbanks arose at 4:00 A.M. on Monday, 24 June 1890, in preparation for the long journey to Europe. "At 6 o'clock I kissed our three youngest—Claud (the baby), Ortho, and Leroy while they slept. Then my wife, and bid her good bye." Fairbanks noted with some remorse: "She

Artists at the American Club in Paris. Art Missionary John Hafen is second from the left in the top row, and John B. Fairbanks is on the far right in the row of men seated on chairs.

was very much affected by the parting, but part we must. The rest of our children beginning with the youngest Ervon, Vernon, Nettie and Leo walked to the depot with me. When the train came I bid them goodbye [and] got on the train leaving the darlings standing on the platform with sorrowful faces and tears standing in their eyes."[13]

The train sped towards Provo, where Fairbanks met Lorus Pratt. At Springville, Utah, the next stop, the third missionary, John Hafen, was waiting "with tears in his eyes." The "dry jokes of Brother Pratt soon brought a smile and our look of sorrow soon disappeared."[14] A fourth missionary would later join them. Edwin Evans was set apart on 2 September 1890.

The Church sponsored the art missionaries' studies with the intent that upon their return to Utah they would paint murals in the temple "endowment rooms."

Pratt, Hafen, and Fairbanks arrived in Paris, France, by August 1890 and enrolled in the Julian Academy. Church leaders often wrote letters of encouragement and sent money for their support throughout their stay. On one occasion, George Q. Cannon wrote Lorus Pratt, asking to be remembered to "Brothers Clawson, Fairbanks,

Haag, Harwood, and Evans," other Latter-day Saints studying in France.

[The First Presidency] feel deeply interested in your success. We want you to become good artists, and to avail yourselves of all the advantages which the French government has so liberally put within the reach of students. . . . We want to see our young men qualified in every direction, so that the Lord's name may be glorified and his cause advanced through their labors and their proficiency in all the arts and sciences. . . . You have our prayers that you may be very successful in gaining a knowledge of art. We desire you to have favor in the eyes of the professors and your fellow students, and also to have favor with the Lord.[15]

While the missionaries continued their studies, other missionaries were being sent on assignments in preparation for the completion of the Salt Lake Temple. For example, one aspect of the Church's preparation for the temple's completion was the gathering of genealogical data needed to perform proxy ordinances in the temple for deceased friends and family members. On 13 July 1891, the missionary committee of the church "set apart James F. Woods for a mission to England to gather genealogies."[16] Many other Saints had made similar trips before, but as the temple neared completion, efforts to obtain these vital records increased.

The most important preparation was raising sufficient funds to cover the increasing temple expenditures. In spite of the international and national economic depression, the worst of the century, President Woodruff pushed forward to complete the structure. An estimated one million dollars was collected and spent from April 1889 to April 1893.

The Depression of 1893 lasted some four years—six hundred banks and perhaps fifteen thousand businesses had failed. Stocks decreased in value by several hundred million dollars. The result was that as many as two and a half million people were left unemployed. Money was hard to come by.

Even Church leaders noted in their personal journals the difficulty of obtaining necessary funds to continue the operations of the Church and their own lives. In this perspective, the continued support for such a large budget is all the more remarkable.

During this period of increased activity toward completing the temple, Church leaders were aware that the innovations in design and the more expensive building materials chosen for the sacred structure were stumbling blocks to a few Saints who expected all the temples to look alike and to be built of the same materials. During a meeting at the Tabernacle, Orson F. Whitney said:

People unfamiliar with the progress of the work of God would not understand that we outgrow former conditions, and assume, under the direction of the Lord, new forms, with the underlying principles ever remaining the same. Some people apostatize because we

Temple construction workers labored long hours and often on holidays to ready the temple for dedication.

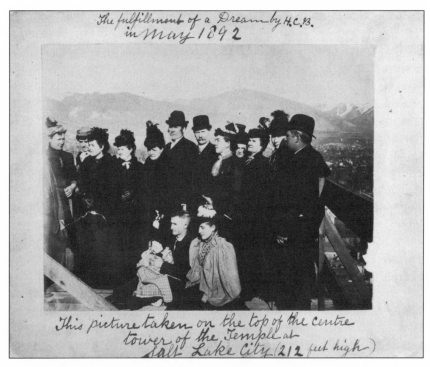

The fulfillment of a Dream by H.C.B. in May 1892

This picture taken on the top of the centre tower of the Temple at Salt Lake City (212 feet high)

Henry Charles Barrell (in the center, looking directly at camera) with group of tourists atop the temple scaffolding, where he served as tour guide and guard.

do not adhere to the old forms, as for instance in the building of the temples in these mountains. President Young had the baptismal fonts made of stone instead of wood as was the case in the days of Joseph; but today we can better afford a more expensive material for our fonts than could be obtained in the days of the Prophet. We must be prepared to accept the word of the Lord as it comes through the man who he appoints to lead.[17]

During the entire period of construction, visitors came from near and far to see the temple. Joseph Kingsbury left his job at the Tithing Office in January 1889 to take a new position across the street as a gatekeeper and guide at the Temple Block.

At his place at the east gate of the Temple Block, Brother Kingsbury greeted friends and visitors, often giving personal tours of the Tabernacle, Assembly Hall, and uncompleted temple. These tours often included an explanation of Latter-day Saint beliefs and the early history of the Saints.

Another brother who obtained employment at the temple site during this period was thankful not only for the opportunity of finding employment but also for the working conditions in the temple structure. On 5 February 1892, he noted in his journal: "I have been to work all day in the temple. [I] like the job real well as it is inside the temple, where the temperature is kept agreeable by steam heaters."[18]

Now that scaffolding had been installed for the towers, many people wanted to ascend the walls of the temple to get a view of the city from the high vantage point. Another local Latter-day Saint was Henry C. Barrell. His story was left on the back of a photograph of himself and a group of tourists visiting the temple. The photograph was taken on "the top of the centre tower of the Temple at Salt Lake City (212 feet high)."[19] Barrell had been out of work for some time and prayed for the Lord's intervention in assisting him to find employment. During the night, he had a dream in which he was bearing his testimony in the midst of a crowd of people and later was by a barrier keeping people back. When he awoke from his dream, he heard a voice saying, "Go to the Temple and ask for work."[20]

Brother Barrell went to the temple, where he found no available work. But the same voice spoke again. Brother Barrell asked if they did not want "anyone to guard some place." Charles Livingston said, "Yes! You are the very man that will guard on top of the tower as we are going to open it to the public."[21] Visitors were required to obtain a ticket in order to ascend the scaffolding. President Woodruff noted, "I gave several permits to go on to the Temple Tower."[22] The view from the top of the temple was tremendous. Several visitors brought binoculars with them, and photographers took pictures of tourists and of the city during this period from atop the temple.

On 16 March 1892, just three weeks before the capstone-laying ceremonies, Professor Charles William Elliot, president of Harvard University, and his wife visited the Temple Block and took advantage of the tour up to the temple towers. Following a special dinner in their honor, the Elliots were escorted to the Tabernacle by President Woodruff. President Woodruff wrote: "We had the organ played and music by the choir. I introduced Professor Elliot to the assembly, who spoke about forty-five minutes in a beautiful and pleasing manner and advocated the rights of all people to the free enjoyment of all religious and political rights. I made a few remarks and returned thanks to Mr. Elliot for his liberal views delivered."[23]

Church leaders were anxious to have such prominent and influential people visit the city and meet the Saints. The temple was always a source of interest for these visitors, and a visit to the site often helped them feel a special spirit. President Woodruff hoped these feelings would be magnified once the temple was completed and dedicated.

When the temple walls were completed, carpenters placed scaffolding up the sides of the towers so the masons could finish laying the stones. Soon, construction on the temple was far enough along to establish a date for the laying of the capstone, the last stone to be placed on the highest east spire. President Wilford Woodruff, along with several other Church leaders, decided on 25 February 1892 that the placing of the capstone of the temple would occur on 6 April 1892, thirty-nine years from the time the cornerstones were laid.

*Salt Lake Temple on 6 April 1892 during
the capstone-laying celebration.*

6

"The Greatest Day the Latter-day Saints Ever Saw"

The completion and dedication of the Salt Lake Temple in 1893 was celebrated enthusiastically and with great display. Nevertheless, excitement ran like a tremor through the Church membership the year before the dedication services. The excitement began with the capstone ceremonies, marking the completion of the stone work on 6 April 1892 when the last stone was officially placed on the building's highest spire.

The weeks preceding the capstone-laying celebration were busy but eventful. The Relief Society celebrated its jubilee—the fifty-year anniversary of its organization by Joseph Smith in Nauvoo, Illinois, on 17 March 1842. On the same day, Andrew Carnegie, the famous "Iron Baron"; Andrew Dickson White, the former president of Cornell University and current president of the New York Chamber of Commerce; and their wives were escorted around Salt Lake City. President Joseph F. Smith and Elders John H. Smith and Abraham H. Cannon "accompanied them to the Temple" and other important sites in the city.[1] Elder Cannon had been busy on the other matters during the week, including the preparation of a pamphlet dealing with the temple.

The Church "temple pamphlet" was made available to the Saints who were visiting Salt Lake City during the capstone-laying activities. The pamphlet was well written and included accounts of ancient and modern temples with illustrations of Latter-day Saint temples. It sold for the "nominal price of ten cents."[2]

Members of the Church began to arrive in Salt Lake City several days before the services commenced. President George Q. Cannon arrived on Saturday from Washington, D.C., where he had been on Church business. From Logan, Utah, Marriner Merrill, an Apostle, arrived with several members of his family on 2 April at 11:20 A.M. The family went to the "Templeton Hotel [and] took room sixty-nine on the sixth floor." The weather was very "stormy and cold," Merrill noted in his journal.[3] Two days later, general conference began in Salt Lake City.

Charles Walker wrote in his journal on 1 April 1892 that "quite a number of the saints in this country [Southern Utah] have gone to April Conference at Salt Lake City to witness the laying of the Capstone." He optimistically noted, "A joyful time is anticipated and favorable weather hoped for."[4] Since the capstone ceremony was an out-of-door activity, the weather was an important concern. President Wilford Woodruff wrote in his journal, "We are having a hard snow storm today," on 30 March, just a few days before the conference began.

Several sessions of conference were held, beginning on Sunday, 3 April. Educational leader and future Apostle James E. Talmage noted that the conference "was a memorable one; and each [Church leader] spoke with the fire of inspiration."[5] As at most conferences, new Church assignments were made, including the calling and sustaining of Jonathan Golden Kimball, son of Heber C. Kimball, to be a member of the First Council of Seventy. Many other administrative meetings were held by Church leaders during the conference period.

The General Authorities of the Church met between conference sessions on 4 April to finalize the capstone-laying service. "At one o'clock the Presidency and Twelve met," Abraham H. Cannon reported, "to consider the program for the exercises at the laying of the capstone of the temple on the 6th."

Elders Heber J. Grant, John W. Taylor, Anthon H. Lund, and Abraham H. Cannon were appointed by the First Presidency to oversee the service and make final physical arrangements for the special meeting. Following the conclusion of the afternoon session of conference, the committee left the Tabernacle and "ascended the scaffolding to the top [of the temple] and had an excellent view of the country. After giving the matter consideration we decided that the best place for the people to stand and for the platform to be erected was on the south side of the Temple."[6]

While it had generally been necessary to hold overflow meetings in the Assembly Hall during weekend conference sessions, previous weekday conference services had been easily accommodated in the Tabernacle alone. However, the special na-

ture of the 1892 April conference changed all of that, and on Tuesday, 5 April, the Tabernacle was full. Jesse W. Crosby reported that it was the "first overflow meeting on a week day that ever occurred in the history of the Church."[7] A report in the *Deseret Evening News* noted that the Tuesday night priesthood meeting was "probably the largest gathering of this kind that has ever convened in the history of the Church in this dispensation."[8] This was only a prelude to the following day's meeting attendance.

On the concluding day of the Church's annual conference in Salt Lake City, 6 April 1892, thousands of people came together to witness the momentous event of the laying of the capstone on the Great Temple. The gathering itself was quite dramatic. Salt Lake City was overflowing; every available room was taken, and in their own homes the Saints bid the visitors welcome as much as was possible. "As soon as the temple block gates were opened the multitude pressed in and filled the Tabernacle," one participant noted. The aisles and

Temple Block during capstone-laying ceremony on 6 April 1892.

doorways of the Tabernacle were full, and "the space surrounding the Tabernacle was filled and thousands more unable to get near enough to hear anything went into the temple yard and got in position to witness the ceremonies that should be conducted there when the Tabernacle services should be ended."[9]

At 10:00 A.M., the morning session of the conference began in the Tabernacle. At the close of the session, President George Q. Cannon said that "in order that there may be no misunderstanding about the manner in which the shout of Hosanna should be given when the capstone should be laid, Pres. Lorenzo Snow would drill the congregation in the shout." President Snow then "instructed the congregation in regard to the shouting of Hosanna, when the stone of the temple shall have been laid."[10]

President Snow said on the occasion, "This is no ordinary order, but is—and we wish it to be distinctly understood—a sacred shout, and employed only on extraordinary occasions like the one now before us." He continued his instruction, "We wish the Saints to feel when they pronounce this shout that it comes from their hearts. Let your hearts be filled with thanksgiving."

President Snow concluded his talk with the admonition, "Now when we go before the temple and this shout goes forth, we want every man and every woman to shout these words to the very extent of their voice, so that every house in this city may tremble, the people in every portion of this city hear it and it may reach to the eternal worlds."[11]

President Snow told the congregation that the sacred shout "was given in the heavens when 'all the sons of God shouted for joy' [Job 38:7]."[12] B. H. Roberts wrote concerning this shout, reserved almost exclusively for such special occasions:

When voiced by thousands and sometimes tens of thousands in unison, and at their utmost strength, it is most impressive and inspiring. It is impossible to stand unmoved on such an occasion. It seems to fill [the site] with mighty waves of sound; and the shout of men going into battle cannot be more stirring. It gives wonderful vent to religious emotions, and is followed by a feeling of reverential awe—a sense of oneness with God.[13]

The priesthood quorums were arranged in order and prepared to march in line to the temple. At the close of the meeting in the Tabernacle, the procession, which was led by a band, gathered to the south side of the temple. The "Temple Anthem" was sung by the congregation; and the author, Charles Walker, who was not present on the occasion, recorded the complete composition in his diary on the day it was sung:

Glorious God, Eternal Father,
In the name of Christ we pray.
Thou wilt bless us with Thy presence,
While this crowning Stone we lay.

Let Thy favor rest upon it,
Let Thy hand protect these towers;
May thy peace brood o'er this Temple.

It is Thine Oh God not ours,
It is Thine, It is Thine,
It's Thine, O God, not ours.

Glory, Glory, Hallelujah!
Heaven and earth, and Angels sing,
Heav'n and earth and Angels sing.
Choirs celestial join the chorus,
Glory be to Christ our King.

Shout hosanna, Shout hosanna!
Glory be to God our head,
For His everlasting mercies
To the living, and the dead;

Joy now reigns where once was sadness
'Midst the prison's dreadful gloom;
Millions hail with joy and gladness,
Victory over hell and tomb!
Victory, victory, victory over hell and tomb.

Sound throughout His vast creations
All His wondrous heavenly host,
Glory be to God the Father,
Jesus Christ, and Holy Ghost;

Sing, ye bright seraphic legions,
Loud as thunder in the sky;
Pealing through celestial regions,
Glory be to God on high.
Glory, Glory, Glory be to God on high.

"How it sounded [at the ceremony] I know not," Walker confided in his journal, since he was unable to attend. "I must here say," he also wrote, "that the repetition of the last line of the verses is the work of the chief chorister to better suit his musical composition and the second verse I intended as chorus."[14] Some fifty thousand people were reportedly in attendance at this special occasion on the Temple Block, with thousands more watching from adjoining rooftops, windows, and even power poles. The streets near the temple were filled with those seeking to witness the exercises of that day. "There was such a jam of humanity, however, that everyone was nearly crushed," Joseph Dean noted. "The whole block was one mass of humanity. After the people had gotten in place as well as they could the ceremonies began."[15] It was the largest gathering in Utah history, a record unchallenged for several decades.

A platform from which the services were conducted had been erected on the south side of the massive granite structure, making a noble background for the Church leaders to conduct the service. Of the current Church officers in 1892, only four of them had been General Authorities when the cornerstones were laid in 1853.

To the left of the main stand was a platform occupied by the Tabernacle Choir. Near the southeast corner of the position occupied by the General Authorities was another stand. This platform was occupied by Evans Stephens, conductor, and Joseph Daynes, organist. All three stands were decorated with national bunting.

The laying-of-the-capstone service began at noon with music, including both band and choir presentations. The weather in Salt Lake City turned pleasant for the festivities: a gentle, warm breeze occasionally passed over the multitude as-

Copper plate placed in temple capstone during special services.

sembled. President George Q. Cannon showed the congregation a polished brass plate inscribed with historical data concerning the temple construction, and the phrase "HOLINESS TO THE LORD." This plate and various Church publications, the standard works, photographs of Church leaders, and various Latter-day Saint coins were laid in with the capstone.[16]

President Joseph F. Smith offered the invocation. Following a hymn, Church architect Joseph

Don Carlos Young shouted from the top of the temple to President Woodruff, "The capstone is now ready to be laid!"[17]

The aged Church leader "stepped to the front of the platform, in full sight of the assembled multitudes, in whose midst a solemn stillness reigned."[18] Excitement ran through the assembled people as President Woodruff, with uplifted hands, announced: "Attention all ye house of Israel, and all ye nations of the earth! We will now lay the

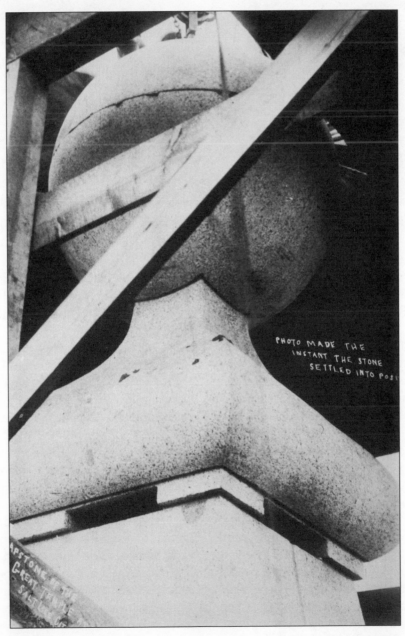

Photograph of capstone: "Photo made the instant the stone settled into position."

Photograph from broken glass negative: "The multitude as seen from the tower during the services of laying the capstone of the temple."

top-stone of the Temple of our God, the foundation of which was laid and dedicated by the Prophet, Seer, and Revelator, Brigham Young."[19]

"The act of laying the stone was performed by President Woodruff," James E. Talmage wrote, "through the agency of electricity, the stone being suspended above its place, and, as the venerable President pressed the button, a catch was released, and the top-most stone of the Temple fell into position.[20] For Emmeline B. Wells, the use of electricity in the endeavor was a "wonderful discovery of science."[21]

When this highest granite block of the temple was in place, President Lorenzo Snow led the Saints in the sacred Hosanna Shout: "Hosanna! Hosanna! Hosanna! to God and the Lamb! Amen! Amen! Amen!"

This heartfelt thanksgiving praise was repeated three times with increasing force as the participants waved white handkerchiefs in the air, except when the names of God and the Lamb were uttered. "The spectacle and effect of this united demonstra-

tion," wrote one witness, "was grand beyond description, the emotions of the multitude being stirred up by it to the greatest intensity of devotion and enthusiasm."[22]

John Lingren, who was visiting Salt Lake City from Idaho Falls, Idaho, recalled: "The scene . . . [was] beyond the power of language to describe. . . . The eyes of thousands were moistened with tears in the fullness of their joy. The ground seemed to tremble with the volume of the sound which sent forth its echoes to the surrounding hills."[23] Another eyewitness wrote, "Everyone shouted as loud as they possibly could waving their handkerchiefs, the effect was indescribable."[24]

The congregation and choir then joined together in singing one of the Church's most soul-stirring hymns, "The Spirit of God Like a Fire Is Burning," originally sung at the first temple dedication on 26 March 1836 in Kirtland, Ohio. Nonmembers of the Church in attendance were impressed with the experience, Joseph Dean wrote, especially as the "united enthusiasm of the teeming thousands visible in every direction from the central stand, in fact reaching far beyond sight or hearing . . . when the choir led out and was sustained by tens of thousands of voices and hearts, unitedly pouring out with unmistakable feeling to the familiar tune."[25]

"When the great song, 'The Spirit of God Like a Fire Is Burning' was sung by the united audience," well-known Utah photographer and Tabernacle Choir member Charles R. Savage wrote, "a different feeling thrilled through me from any one I have ever experienced. The hosannah shout was something long to be remembered and one I never expect to hear again during my life."[26]

The Union Glee Club next rendered a selection prepared especially for the ceremony, entitled "The Temple Ode."

All hail this glorious day,
This grand, auspicious day.
The vales resound, the mountains ring,
The capstone on the Temple bring,
With gladsome peal, united sing,
Of truth's still widening way.

The time is near at hand,
When Christ shall come and claim His own.
And 'mid his Saints erect that throne,
Which on the earth must stand.

All hail that glorious day,
The shadows melt away;
The skies are bright,
Soon truth and right,
Shall come to earth from Zion's light.
And man redeemed at last shall shine,
Our Father's image, all divine.

Francis M. Lyman of the Quorum of the Twelve proposed a resolution to those gathered that they "pledge themselves, collectively and individually, to furnish, as fast as it may be needed, all the money that may be required to complete the temple at the earliest time possible, so that the dedication may take place on April 6th, 1893."[27] John Dean reported that the result was "a deafening shout of 'ayes' from the assembled host" as they raised their right hands.[28] A subscription list was then presented, with Lyman at the top of the list, pledging one thousand dollars.

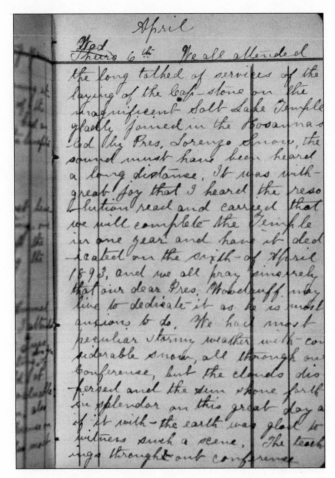

Mary Ann Burnham Freeze diary entry for
6 April 1892.

Mary Ann Freeze said it was "with great joy that I heard the resolution read and carried that we will complete the temple in one year and we all prayed sincerely that our dear President Woodruff may live to dedicate it as he is most anxious to do so."[29]

For several Saints, a more personal and individual manifestation of the Spirit was present during the services. For instance, Christina Willardson of Manti "saw a halo of light around one of the brethren when speaking."[30]

Following the singing of a hymn, "Song of the Redeemed," President George Q. Cannon offered the benediction, and the ceremony ended. Abraham H. Cannon noted in his journal, "It was scarcely possible to get around in the immense crowd of people who thronged the streets this afternoon." Nevertheless, "everybody's heart seems full of thanksgiving and praise," noted Joseph Henry Dean.[31]

L. John Nuttall, a private secretary to President Woodruff, "had a good seat on the platform, to hear and see all that was going on." For him, "this had been an eventful day. I saw the foundation stones of the Temple laid, and today [I] witnessed the laying of the capstone."[32]

John Nicholson, the official conference clerk, wrote: "The entire scene was imposing, presenting a spectacle that has not been duplicated on this continent in modern times. It must have made an impression to people who witnessed—especially the participants in the ceremonies—that will never be effaced from their memory."[33]

Following the services, workers prepared the building for the placement of several more items—the angel Moroni statue, ornamental spires, and electrical lights. William Jeffs, who had worked "on the Temple as [the] hoisting engineer" since 1891, raised not only "the last rock—the capstone, [but] also Moroni, the statue," he noted in his journal.[34] Work on the angel Moroni statue started several years earlier when Church authorities contracted the famous sculptor, Cyrus E. Dallin.

The Utah-born Dallin had been asked by President Wilford Woodruff to make the statue representing the angel Moroni for the temple, but Dallin declined, stating that he was not a Mormon and "didn't believe in angels." He felt someone of greater spiritual capacity should be given the opportunity. Undeterred, President Woodruff asked him to reconsider and to consult with his mother, whom Dallin was completely devoted to, in Springville, Utah.

Jane Dallin, a gentle, religiously devout individual, believed that her son should accept the commission. When Cyrus argued that his lack of belief in angels prevented him from taking the assignment, his mother countered, "Every time you return home and take me in your arms you call me your 'angel mother.'"[35] He accepted the commission and began a study of Latter-day Saint scriptures and doctrine in an effort to truly interpret Moroni's character. Besides the writings of Joseph Smith, Dallin felt that John's vision in the New Testament book of Revelation gave him the necessary feeling for the demeanor of the angel: "And I

George Albert Smith and Ephraim Holding (temple electrician), installing lights on temple spires.

saw another angel fly in the midst of heaven, having the everlasting gospel to preach unto them that dwell on the earth, and to every nation, and kindred, and tongue, and people" (Revelation 14:6).

Soon, the preliminary sketches were completed and wholeheartedly accepted by President Woodruff. The original plaster model was completed, and by 4 October 1891, following a public exhibition, it was sent to Ohio to W. H. Mullins and Company, who created the statue with hammered copper that was in turn covered with twenty-two-carat gold leaf.

Many remained to see the unveiling of the angel Moroni statue following the completion of the capstone-laying ceremony. Before nightfall, the massive gold-leafed figure was lowered into position on the stone ball of the 210-foot-high central east spire. The crowd below, including President Wilford Woodruff and Cyrus E. Dallin, watched in awe. It is reported that President Woodruff turned to Dallin and asked, "Now, Mr. Dallin, do you believe in angels?" His response was, "Yes, my mother is an angel."[36]

A four-hundred-candle-power electrical lamp was placed on the top of the statue (on the crown of the head) for illumination, and on the following evening functioned for the first time. The ornamental spires and electrical lights were then placed on the five other towers.[37]

Jane Blood, with her husband, George, "went up on the temple right up to the angel and touched it. We put a dime each through a hole in the capstone" and returned home to Bountiful, Utah, late in the evening.[38] On the following day, Emmeline B. Wells reported that "many people are

The statue of the angel Moroni atop the capstone. Note the electrical wires up the statue's back and the light socket on its head which were used to illuminate the statue until 1930.

climbing up to the tower of the temple, hundreds of them in fact, strangers, gentiles and Jews, as well as our own [people]."[39]

The walls were washed and received the finishing touches. The scaffolding was gradually removed, leaving the exterior building completed, with nothing to mar the sight and study of its magnificent beauty.

The capstone-laying ceremony was an important moment for the Saints as they prepared to complete the temple. For those who had been present thirty-nine years earlier when the first cornerstones were laid, the moment was a long-awaited event. President Wilford Woodruff, who had been present when the site was first selected and consecrated in 1853, noted in his journal:

> This was the most interesting day, in some respects, the Church has ever seen since its organization. The Temple capstone was laid with imposing ceremonies with electricity by [me]. . . . It was the largest assembly I ever saw meet on any occasion of the Latter-day Saints. . . . This was certainly the greatest day the Latter-day Saints ever saw in these mountains.[40]

Now that the capstone was laid, preparations to complete and dedicate the House of the Lord in Salt Lake City began. Indeed, Church leaders met on the day following the capstone-laying ceremonies, during which time the "First Presidency occupied most of the time in speaking on the Temple."[41]

From the time the capstone was laid, an intense effort was made by carpenters, painters, plasterers, and other skilled craftsmen, who took great care in completing the interior of the temple for dedication. They adorned it with fine wood and plaster ornamental carvings, beautiful murals and paintings, mirrors, elegant curtains and draperies, the best carpets and furniture available, and fine light fixtures and chandeliers. Specially ordered stained glass art windows from Tiffany and Company in New York depicting various scriptural stories were installed.[42] Painstakingly, yet with all possible haste, all things were made ready for the dedication ceremonies, which were to begin on 6 April 1893.

AN ADDRESS.

To the Officers and Members of the Church of Jesus Christ of Latter-day Saints:

The near approach of the date for the dedication of the Temple of our God moves us to express with some degree of fullness our feelings to our brethren, the officers of the Church who with us bear the Priesthood of the Son of God, and to the Latter-day Saints generally; to the end that in entering into that holy building we may all be found acceptable ourselves, with our households, and that the building which we shall dedicate may also be acceptable unto the Lord.

The Latter-day Saints have used their means freely to erect other Temples in these valleys, and our Father has blessed us in our efforts. Today we enjoy the great happiness of having three of these sacred structures completed, dedicated to and accepted of the Lord, wherein the Saints can enter and attend to those ordinances which He, in His infinite goodness and kindness, has revealed. But for forty years the hopes, desires, and anticipations of the entire Church have been centered upon the completion of this edifice in the principal city of Zion. Its foundation was laid in the early days of our settlement in these mountains; and from that day until the present, the eyes of the members of the Church in every land have been lovingly directed toward it. Looking upon it as the Temple of Temples, the people during all these years have labored with unceasing toil, undiminished patience and ungrudging expenditure of means to bring it to its present condition of completion; and now that the toils and the sacrifices of forty years are crowned so successfully and happily; now that the great building is at last finished and ready to be used for divine purposes, need we say that we draw near an event whose consummation is to us as a people momentous in the highest degree? Far-reaching in its consequences as that occasion is certain to be, what remains for us to say in order to impress the entire Church with a sense of its tremendous importance!

On this point, surely nothing; yet may we offer a few words upon a phase that directly touches it. No member of the Church who would be deemed worthy to enter that sacred house can be considered ignorant of the principles of the Gospel. It is not too much to presume that every one knows what his duty is to God and to his fellow man. None is so forgetful as to have lost sight of the admonition that we must be filled with love for and charity toward our brethren. And hence none can for a moment doubt the supreme importance of every member of the congregation being at peace with all his or her brethren and sisters, and at peace with God. How else can we hope to gain the blessings He has promised save by complying with the requirements for which those blessings are the reward!

Can men and women who are violating a law of God, or those who are derelict in yielding obedience to His commands, expect that the mere going into His holy house and taking part in its dedication will render them worthy to receive, and cause them to receive, His blessing?

Do they think that repentance and turning away from sin may be so lightly dispensed with?

Do they dare, even in thought, thus to accuse our Father of injustice and partiality, and attribute to Him carelessness in the fulfillment of His own words?

Assuredly no one claiming to belong to His people would be guilty of such a thing.

Then must those who are unworthy cease to expect a blessing from their attendance at the Temple while sin unrepented of still casts its odor about them, and while bitterness or even an unforgiving coolness exists in their hearts against their brethren and sisters.

On this latter subject we feel that much might be said. In the striving after compliance with the apparently weightier matters of the law, there is a possibility that the importance of this spirit of love and kindness and charity may be underestimated. For ourselves, we cannot think of any precept that at present requires more earnest inculcation.

During the past eighteen months there has been a division of the Latter-day Saints upon national party lines. Political campaigns have been conducted, elections have been held, and feelings, more or less intense, have been engendered in the minds of brethren and sisters upon one side and the other.

We have been cognizant of conduct and have heard of many expressions that have been very painful to us and have grieved our spirits.

We know they have been an offense unto the God of peace and love, and a stumbling-block unto many of the Saints.

We feel now that a time for reconciliation has come; that before entering into the Temple to present ourselves before the Lord in solemn assembly, we shall divest ourselves of every harsh and unkind feeling against each other; that not only our bickerings shall cease, but that the cause of them shall be removed, and every sentiment that prompted and has maintained them shall be dispelled; that we shall confess our sins one to another, and ask forgiveness one of another; that we shall plead with the Lord for the spirit of repentance, and, having obtained it, follow its promptings; so that in humbling ourselves before Him and seeking forgiveness from each other, we shall yield that charity and generosity to those who crave our forgiveness that we ask for and expect from Heaven.

Thus may we come up into the holy place with our hearts free from guile and our souls prepared for the edification that is promised! Thus shall our supplications, undisturbed by a thought of discord, unitedly mount into the ears of Jehovah and draw down the choice blessings of the God of Heaven!

As your brethren, sustained by your vote and in your faith as the First Presidency of the Church, we have this to say to the Latter-day Saints, in our individual as well as our official capacity: If there is a single member of the Church who has feelings against us, we do not wish to cross the threshold of the Temple until we have satisfied him and removed from him all cause of feeling, either by explanation or by making proper amends and atonement; neither would we wish to enter the sacred portals of that edifice until we have sought an explanation, or amends, or atonement from any against whom we may have either a real or fancied grievance.

In now announcing this course for ourselves, we say to all the other officers of the Church that we desire them to follow our example. We wish them from highest to lowest and throughout all the Stakes and Wards of Zion to take heed of this counsel. Let them invite all who may have feelings against them to come forward and make them known; let them then endeavor to correct any misapprehensions or misunderstandings which may exist, or give redress for any wrong or injury that may have been done.

We say the same—and when the officers have taken the course indicated we wish them to say the same—to the individual members of the Church. We call upon them to seek to have the fellowship of their brethren and their sisters, and their entire confidence and love; above all to seek to have the fellowship and union of the Holy Ghost. Let this spirit be sought and cherished as diligently within the the smallest and humblest family circle as within the membership of the highest organization and quorum. Let it permeate the hearts of the brothers and sisters, the parents and children of the household, as well as the hearts of the First Presidency and Twelve. Let it mellow and soften all differences between members of the Stake Presidencies and the High Councils, as well as between neighbors living in the same ward. Let it unite young and old, male and female, flock and shepherd, people and Priesthood in the bonds of gratitude and forgiveness and love, so that Israel may feel approved of the Lord, and that we may all come before Him with a conscience void of offense before all men. Then there will be no disappointment as to the blessings promised those who sincerely worship Him. The sweet whisperings of the Holy Spirit will be given to them and the treasures of Heaven, the communion of angels, will be ad led from time to time, for His promise has gone forth and it cannot fail!

Asking God's blessing upon you all in your endeavor to carry out this counsel, and desirous of seeing it take the form of a united effort on the part of the whole people, we suggest that Saturday, March 25th, 1893, be set apart as a day of fasting and prayer. On that occasion we advise that the Presidencies of Stakes, the High Councils, the Bishops and their Counselors, meet together with the Saints in their several meeting houses, confess their sins one to another, and draw out from the people all feelings of anger, of distrust, or of unfriendliness that may have found a lodgment; so that entire confidence may then and there be restored and love from this time prevail through all the congregations of the Saints.

WILFORD WOODRUFF,
GEORGE Q. CANNON,
JOSEPH F. SMITH,

First Presidency of the Church of Jesus Christ of Latter-day Saints.

N. B.—Dear Brother: Please give this all possible publicity

First Presidency letter: "An Address to the Officers and Members of the Church of Jesus Christ of Latter-day Saints," March 1893.

7

"That . . . We May All Be Found Acceptable"

A few days following the capstone-laying ceremony, President Woodruff, his wife, Emma, and two daughters went to the temple: "[We] were drawn up to the top tower in an elevator, myself and family. We all put a dime apiece into the [capstone]. We went through every room in the house. We saw a great deal of work yet to be done in order to get the [temple] done by next April Conference."[1]

President Woodruff returned to the temple four days later on 15 April to encourage the workers. Abraham H. Cannon recorded: "We spoke to the workmen about our desires that the building should be finished by the 6th of April next. We requested all to use their best endeavors to crowd the work ahead, and to refrain from evil conversation [and] discussion of politics."[2]

Three days later, the First Presidency took time to write a letter to the art missionaries still remaining in France:

> We shall have the rooms selected that we wish to have artistically decorated, and shall do all in our power to have the walls put in a suitable condition for the work. . . . We would be pleased to have you return home in time to spend the fall and winter months in finishing the Temple. It may be that you would be pleased to have the size of the rooms given you that we wish artistic work put upon, and also the character of the painting and then if you were furnished with these you might be able to get your designs to better advantage there.

The Presidency concluded the letter, "We would like to get the benefit of the best artistic skill now in the Church in the decoration of this grand building."[3]

As the art missionaries prepared to come home, other workers began working on the ornamental detail for the interior of the building. On 22 April 1892, Samuel Richards "went to the Temple block and Brother Cox, the Superintendent offered me a job at carving work," he wrote. Richards was somewhat surprised since he "was not acquainted with that class of business."[4] However, Richards took the position and began his labors on 3 May.

Richards worked on the "pilasters for the terrestrial room" and other areas in the temple.[5] In September, Richards and his fellow woodcarvers met at the temple site for a photograph: "September 12, 1892—Monday at shop work all day on leaf carving for circle doorheads. Obtained picture of the carvers and their work for the temple taken by artist Olsen (75 cents)."[6]

While the work continued at the Temple Block, other efforts to assist were enacted by general and local Church officers, in particular the collection of the necessary funds for construction costs. Church officers called for a special Church-wide fast in May 1892, the fast offerings collected to be used for the temple.

In Logan, Elder Marriner Merrill attended the local ward fast and testimony meeting. He noted in his journal: "May 1—Sunday. At home. I attended the general fast meeting, which was general throughout the whole Church. Meeting held from

Temple carvers standing in front of temple heating plant. Samuel W. Richards, upper right, is holding a decorative piece for the terrestrial room.

10 a.m. until 2 p.m. A subscription was taken up to finish the Salt Lake Temple, and $625.00 was subscribed and $58.00 cash was paid. I subscribed $100.00."[7]

Back in Salt Lake City, the Saints did the same. Abraham H. Cannon wrote, "From all I was able to hear of other wards in this city their meetings were all crowded, and the amounts subscribed to the Temple fund were large." Furthermore "myself nor any of my family partook of food," and each family member handed him a contribution for the temple fund, amounting to a total of one hundred and thirteen dollars.[8]

The Cannons attended the Salt Lake City Fifth Ward meeting. The house was "packed to its utmost capacity" for the three-and-a-half-hour service, which time "was mostly occupied in the bearing of testimony." At the conclusion of the meeting, the "people gave freely, I think, according to their means" for the completion of the temple.[9]

In August the Twelve Apostles met with the First Presidency at the President's office. "The matter of dedicating the Salt Lake temple next April was considered," Elder Cannon reported.[10] The first order of business was the decision to push

forward in completing the temple by 6 April 1893. "We agreed," Wilford Woodruff noted, "to dedicate the temple at Salt Lake next April. We concluded to hold two meetings a day in the temple and read the dedicatory prayer and speeches at each meeting."[11] Elder Cannon recorded: "It was decided after all the brethren had spoken to hold the exercises in the temple each day until every worthy member of the Church should have the privilege of entering into the building and taking part in the dedicatory exercises."[12]

During the Church's semiannual conference in the fall of 1892, several conference speakers emphasized the desire to complete the temple. President Joseph F. Smith of the First Presidency spoke "for forty-five minutes" during the Friday 7 October session. Among those topics addressed were temple offerings for the completion of the temple.[13] As the Saints received encouragement to continue their efforts to provide the necessary funds to complete the temple, the workers themselves were busily engaged just a few hundred feet from the Tabernacle. The interior woodcarvers were so anxious to complete their work on time that they decided "to continue work on the temple rather than attend the conference meetings in the Tabernacle."[14] Three days later at 10:00 A.M., Church authorities met in the large, unfinished assembly room with stake presidents and bishops. L. John Nuttall reported:

> President George Q. Cannon made a few opening remarks on the erection of the Temple, etc. Bishop John H. Winder read a financial statement of receipts and disbursements for the temple. Pres. Woodruff spoke. President George Q. Cannon moved that the brethren present make every possible exertion themselves and among the people to raise the necessary funds to complete this temple. . . . It was represented that there are five large windows needed which will cost $1500.00 each. Brothers John R. Winder, Moses Thatcher, George Romney, Heber J. Grant, and John R. Murdock agreed to each furnish one window. . . . On motion a few of the brethren were requested to take the names and amounts which each one present felt to give to the completion

of the Temple. $50,000.00 was subscribed at this meeting.[15]

"There was a good attendance and the spirit which prevailed was heavenly," Abraham H. Cannon stated. At the close of the meeting in the upper assembly room, "we were all shown through the Temple and saw the fine workmanship which is being done."[16] Church architect Joseph Don Carlos Young sent a letter to artist Dan Weggeland on 21 October 1892, stating in part, "At a meeting with the First Presidency yesterday it was decided to call a committee of our home artists to take up the work of painting in the garden and the world [rooms], and go ahead as rapidly as possible, as the time is now short, there only being five months yet before dedication."[17]

Other Utah artists, including John Hafen and John Fairbanks, received copies of the letters requesting their help at the temple. The proposed murals were designed to enhance the interior decoration of the temple and therefore intensify the endowment experience of the participant. The design of the temple's interior allowed several rooms to be decorated with murals—the creation room, the Garden of Eden room, and the telestial room. John Hafen arrived home first from Europe, where he had been serving as an art missionary. He and the other art missionaries began their work on the murals as soon as they arrived home. President Woodruff met with several artists on 12 January 1893: "[I] met with the artists for painting in the temple. They asked seventeen thousand dollars for painting two rooms. We could not pay that price. We finally agreed to give them three hundred dollars a month."[18]

Two rooms—the garden room and the telestial room (world room)—were completed in time for the dedication in 1893. Over the next few years, the art missionaries completed the other rooms in the temple.

"The delicate task of beautifying the [garden room] and [telestial room] . . . was performed by local artists, Dan Weggeland, John Hafen, Lorus Pratt, John B. Fairbanks, and Edwin Evans," an article stated. The garden room was "luminous with warm and natural effects in landscape, beasts and birds." The telestial room "is gorgeously frescoed,

Preliminary sketch (1892) for garden room mural.

and in its harmony of coloring and accuracy of drawing is as enchanting as a dream."[19]

In an effort to complete the temple on time, workers continued their labors even on holidays. On Thanksgiving Day, 24 November 1892, "nearly all the men were at work as usual," one worker wrote.[20]

Just a few days before the end of the year, a Church member named William H. Shearman died following a brief illness. Following his funeral Abraham H. Cannon reflected, "He was a very liberal man, and the day of his death I received from him a letter containing the amount of over $150.00 in a note of Godbe-Pitts Drug Co., payable in 60 days, to be applied on a donation to the temple in this city."[21] As was evident from this act, the completion of the temple was a major concern of all Saints, not just of the leading Brethren.

The year 1893 began with Church leaders busily engaged in preparing for the temple dedication. As donations were received to the temple fund, letters of appreciation were sent to the donors and their respective local Church leaders. On 1 January 1893, Heber J. Grant wrote Bishop John C. Sharp at Vernon, Utah:

Dear Friend: Brother Pehrson has sent me $238.00 as an additional donation to the Temple and I have just written him a letter of thanks and my blessing. I feel that you as his bishop and the father of the Saints in your ward should extend special thanks to Brother Pehrson and add your blessing to [mine]. . . . I am delighted beyond measure with the hearty and liberal donation, from the leading brethren in the Tooele Stake, to the Temple. Once more wishing you and yours a Happy New Year, I remain Sincerely your friend and brother, Heber J. Grant.[22]

Other Church authorities, including President Woodruff, were engaged in items relating to temple matters. On 3 January, the various contractors met with the First Presidency for three hours to determine completion dates for their work. "Each one was required to tell how long it would take them to finish their parts," President Woodruff wrote. "They all represented they could get their parts done in time for the [planned April] dedication."[23]

President Woodruff's subsequent days were filled with almost daily decision-making meetings on items such as furnishings and expenditures. He himself donated five hundred dollars to the temple construction fund on 6 January. On 25 January he went to the temple to address "the workmen and urged them to finish the Temple by the 6 of April," he reported. In a passionate plea, he said, "If I live and can stand on my feet I expect to go into that temple and dedicate it on the 6 of next April."[24]

Unexpected delays came up during the months preceding the dedication services. On one occasion during a visit to the temple, Church leaders discovered that no provisions had been made for dressing rooms in the temple. President Woodruff was "quite unwell through the night" as a result.[25]

Church architect Joseph Don Carlos Young, who was very sick at the time, offered to resign, if

doing so would hasten the completion of the work. President Woodruff refused and insisted that Young accomplish as much as he could and let others help. A new temple committee, composed of Joseph F. Smith, Lorenzo Snow, and Abraham H. Cannon, was selected to ensure the temple's completion on time.

Abraham H. Cannon, who previously had kept a meticulous daily journal, made an entry on 4 January 1893 and then another on 21 March, approximately a two-and-one-half-month lapse. He wrote:

I feel ashamed for my neglect of the past few weeks in regard to the writing of my journal, but I have been so extremely busy in various ways that it has been impossible for me to find the necessary time in which to do so. . . . I have acted during the time on the committee with Brothers Joseph F. Smith and Lorenzo Snow to see that the temple in this city is finished ready for dedication on April 6th. Our duties in looking after the workmen [have] kept me visiting the building with the other brethren nearly every other day.[26]

President Woodruff was determined to dedicate the temple on 6 April, even though, as he confessed in his journal, "we are in hopes to get it ready for dedication, but it is a load upon us."[27]

On another occasion, President Woodruff came to the temple to talk with the workers. He had heard that some of the workmen believed the temple could not possibly be completed on time. William Hurst recalled, "He said when he looked at this body of men he didn't believe a word of it. Some of you may be sick and weak (I thought he was talking to me)." He continued, "Some of you may give out at night, but you will be here in the morning if you are faithful." President Woodruff told the workers they were "not here by accident. You were ordained in the Eternal World to perform this work. Brethren, I will be here April 6th to dedicate this building."[28] For many, this insight from the Prophet led them to be diligent and prompt in their efforts to complete the temple on schedule.

President Woodruff asked Elder Franklin D.

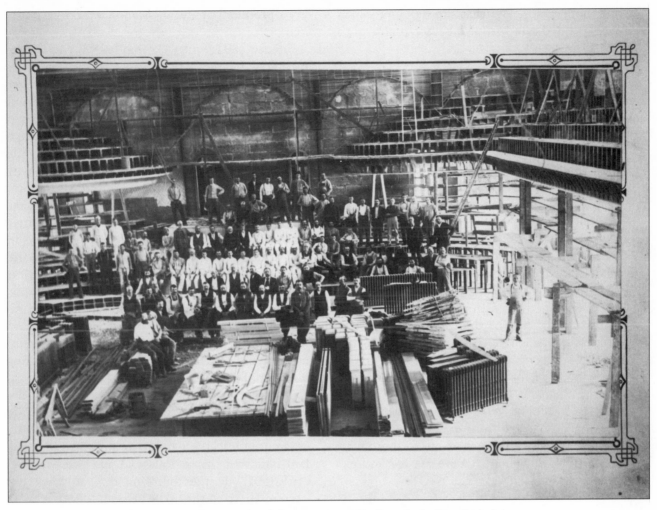

Temple workers completed the upper assembly floor, including the balcony,
in preparation for the dedication services held in this room.

Richards and others to draft the dedication prayer for the occasion. On 17 March President Woodruff, along with his counselors, "read over the dedication prayer and made some additions to it."[29] Once completed, the prayer would be read in each session of the dedication, then printed and distributed for publication following the first dedication service on 6 April.

In anticipation of the temple dedication, the Union Pacific Railroad Company published a twenty-four-page booklet announcing the event and advertising the railroad's passenger routes to Salt Lake City for those interested in attending the services. Reduced rates and additional schedules were available to tourists and visitors. The brochure presented a positive image of the Church and of Utah.[30]

The Saints themselves prepared spiritually as they observed a special fast day. On 18 March 1893, the Church's First Presidency issued an epistle to Church members:

The near approach of the date for the dedication of the Temple of our God moves us to express with some degree of fulness our feelings to our brethren, the officers of the Church, who with us bear the Priesthood of the Son of God, and to the Latter-day Saints generally; to the end that in entering that holy building we may all be found acceptable ourselves, with our households, and that the building which we shall dedicate may also be acceptable unto the Lord.[31]

Church leaders were concerned that the Saints exhibit a new feeling of unity and spiritual purity during the special season of rejoicing so that the Spirit of the Lord would be among them during the dedication services. The epistle continued:

We feel now that a time for reconciliation has come; that before entering into the Temple to present ourselves before the Lord in solemn assembly, we shall divest ourselves of every harsh and unkind feeling against each other; that not only our bickerings shall cease, but that the cause of them shall be removed, and every sentiment that prompted and has maintained them shall be dispelled; that we shall confess our sins one to another, and ask forgiveness one of another; that we shall plead with the Lord for the spirit of repentance, and having obtained it, follow its promptings; so that in humbling ourselves before Him and seeking forgiveness from each other, we shall yield that charity and generosity to those who crave our forgiveness that we ask for and expect from Heaven.[32]

Church officers blessed and encouraged the Saints in this effort to purge themselves of the human frailties that so often beset mortals: "Asking God's blessing upon you all in your endeavor to carry out this counsel, and desirous of seeing it take the form of a united effort on the part of the whole people, we suggest that Saturday, March 25, 1893, be set apart as a day of fasting and prayer."[33]

The First Presidency and the Council of the Twelve met in the Historian's Office for their own fast meeting on 23 March, just two days before the general fast day. In the meeting, they decided that only those members of the Church who were in total and complete harmony with the First Presidency would be invited to attend the dedication services. Clearly, Church leaders understood that without a united spirit and perfect harmony among them, the spiritual outpouring that had

been promised at the dedication would be inhibited.

Since 1891, when Church leaders encouraged members of the Church to disband the local People's Party in Utah and to join the organized national parties (Democrat and Republican), some members of the Church had expressed some ill feelings on political issues as some members supported one political party and others another. This disharmony among faithful Saints, along with other problems, was of direct concern to the First Presidency. They hoped that through fasting and prayer, reconciliation would occur and unity would increase among the Saints.

Church leaders attended their own local wards to participate in the general Church fast. Marriner Merrill noted: "I went to the meeting at 11 a.m., met with the people of Richmond, confessed my sins, and asked forgiveness of the Saints. . . . Many of the Saints, male and female, spoke in a similar manner. We had an excellent meeting; held it four hours until all were satisfied."[34]

During a meeting he attended, Henry Ballard said the Saints voted "to forgive each other." The Saints reached out to former members who were readmitted into the Church as a result. Elder Ballard indicated that a "husband and wife were reconfirmed" on the following day, as "they had been re-baptized the night before."[35]

During one meeting, "there was a great out pouring of the spirit of God" and the "gifts of the spirit" were manifested in a special way among the congregation. Mary Ann Freeze's sister, Lillie, "sang in tongues," and Mary M. Morris "had the interpretation." The people were filled with a "humble, repentant, child-like spirit" during the entire meeting.[36]

Similar fast day meetings were observed "throughout Utah which [did] a great deal of good," President Woodruff wrote in his diary.[37]

Shortly thereafter, on 30 March 1893, the First Council of the Seventy met in the temple for a special meeting. Elder B. H. Roberts wrote, "On entering the room a pleasing sense of gratitude filled my heart of the privileges thus accorded to our council [that] we should here have the privilege of meeting in council and prayer."[38] The purpose of the meeting was to allow the Brethren to express their own feelings and ensure perfect harmony.

On the same day, the First Presidency met with a prominent lay member of the Church who had come to discuss the differences he had with the Presidency during the past year. "He confessed and asked forgiveness," President Woodruff noted.[39] To President Woodruff's satisfaction, the reconciliation he had prayed for was taking place among the Saints.

Before the dedication services began, special issues of Church magazines and newspapers were published to help the Saints prepare for the day. For the young women, an article entitled "Etiquette" was published in the *Young Woman's Journal*. The essay, devoted to teaching the young sisters proper behavior at the dedication services, indicated that "all eyes are turned towards the Salt Lake Temple, and all hearts are set upon its dedication."[40]

The young women were directed to "lay aside all levity of feeling" when entering the portals of the temple. They were requested to "refrain from all unnecessary talk. Train your eyes to see and observe minutely. Take in silently, reverently, the beauties and perfection around you." They were also informed to "be helpful and pleasant" to their host families during their stay in the city and "you will be always welcomed."[41]

While it was certain that "the Lord will accept the offering which His people present in the dedication of the Salt Lake Temple," George Q. Cannon was "not so sure that He will accept all the people."[42] It was hoped, however, that the Saints' spiritual preparation would allow them to be accepted. It now seemed that all was ready for the long-anticipated event.

Saints from Wallsburg, Utah, arriving in
Salt Lake City to participate in the dedication services.

8

"Members of the Church . . . Are Cordially Invited"

The First Presidency announced without fanfare the upcoming conference in newspapers throughout the intermountain west: "The Sixty-third Annual Conference of the Church of Jesus Christ of Latter-day Saints will convene in the Tabernacle, Salt Lake City, at 10 o'clock on Tuesday morning April 4th, 1893. The officers and members of the Church generally are cordially invited to attend."[1]

Local priesthood officers were busy interviewing members for "temple recommend passes" up to the last moment. Bishop David John of Provo noted that as late as 3 April, just three days before the first dedication session, he "was kept busy all day giving recommends to the Saints to attend the dedicatory service."[2]

The Saints began arriving in the city days and weeks before the commencement of general conference. The Associated Press wire services carried this report across the nation: "The throng of visitors in the city was augmented by large delegations arriving on every train. Excursion trains are arriving hourly. The principal streets are packed with visiting saints and visitors from all directions."[3]

Jesse Smith and his family left their home in Arizona on 31 March to begin their long journey to Salt Lake City with some thirty-eight fellow Saints. Brother Smith noted, "Arrangements had been made with the railway companies for a rate of $45 for the round trip."[4] On the train, he met Saints from Mexico traveling to the temple dedication. The train from Colorado Springs was "uncomfortable and dirty," but these conditions did not dampen their spirits as they visited, sang, and discussed topics of interest.[5] The passengers finally reached Salt Lake City four days later, on 4 April, at five o'clock in the evening.

Seventy-four-year-old Benjamin F. Johnson, a resident of Arizona, wrote about his arrival in Salt Lake: "On my midnight arrival at Salt Lake I found my darling niece, Rosemary, and other of my brothers' children waiting to convey me to their home where I was received by their mother and cared for with that degree of kindness."[6] The aged patriarch had been violently ill since 28 March, when it "appeared a greater prospect of my going to the grave than to Salt Lake."[7] Still in poor health, Johnson rejoiced in his safe arrival and the prospects of attending the dedication.

By and large, most people arrived on time and without difficulty on the special trains, but a "Union Pacific Conference train with many passengers was thrown from the track about four miles south of Juab." A broken rail caused the accident, which threw one car off the track and onto its side. Although the people were frightened and several were bruised, no one was seriously hurt, and they experienced only a one-hour delay.[8]

Several train companies offered special discounts and gave away complimentary tickets. The Union Pacific train line "distributed among the poor [of Utah County] two hundred complimentary tickets, besides giving twenty-five extra tickets to the [Provo] Stake authorities."[9] This kind gesture did not, however, meet the needs of all the Saints, especially those who lived long distances from Salt Lake City.

Those who lived near train depots and along railroad lines, but could not afford the cost of passage, made the long trip from their homes on horseback or in wagons. Lucy Flake started on her trip to Utah on 8 March 1893 from Arizona. "We went by team," she noted in her journal, "as we hadn't the money to go on train." The group "consisted of William, myself, Sister Lanning, Joel and John, Henry and Emma Tanner and two of their children," she wrote. The journey by wagon was "a cold hard trip, through snow and mud."[10]

At Beaver, Utah, the Flake family finally boarded a train. "William and I took our first train ride together," Lucy Flake recalled. "We went with a large company of our friends and relatives from Beaver City to Salt Lake. We were joined at every station by others who were going to the Dedication."[11]

The Flakes' final arrival in Salt Lake City was a welcome delight for the weary travelers. They "went right to [her] dear Sister Mary's," Lucy recorded. "She was expecting us and had the supper table all set for us."[12] She, like many other Saints, found room in the homes of family members already living in the city. But finding accommodations was a major problem, and some visitors were forced to camp out at the "tithing grounds."

Many Saints lived in areas not served by the railroads and therefore had to travel to Salt Lake City on horseback or in buggies and wagons. The Saints from Wallsburg, Wasatch County, Utah, came as a group to witness the special activities. Twelve-year-old Grace Greer wrote, "We started out on Monday, April 10th last, to attend the dedication of the Salt Lake Temple."[13]

During the journey, an accident occurred when the family wagon came to a deep ditch in the road. As her father and two younger sisters were being thrown from the wagon, she "asked God to keep" her father and sisters from being killed. The Lord heard her sincere prayer, and the family was able to continue their travels.

From Manti, Utah, Thomas and Elizabeth Higgs came to Salt Lake City not only to participate in the Church conference and temple dedication services but also to visit family members and to attend reunions and local Church ecclesiastical meetings. The Higgs family had been converted in 1856 in Davenport, Iowa, and had journeyed with the William B. Hodgett wagon train and the famous Martin Handcart Company to Utah. The

companies were caught in the early snowstorms in Wyoming, and the participants suffered much from the ordeal. Now, thirty-seven years later, the pioneers met together during the conference to plan a reunion. The *Deseret Evening News* advised these 1856 immigrants of the meeting: "NOTICE TO OLD TIMERS. The old timers who came to the valley in the late companies of 1856, viz: Willies, Martin, Hunt and Hodgett, also those who went from the valley to their rescue, are requested to meet at the Globe Bakery on East Temple Street on Saturday, April 8, at 8 p.m. to make arrangements for a reunion."[14]

Thomas and Elizabeth Higgs attended several dedication sessions. On two occasions, Friday and Saturday, 7-8 April, Brother Higgs sang in the Sanpete County Choir (oftentimes referred to as the Manti Choir) at the services. While in Salt Lake City, Higgs visited with family members who had remained in the city following his move to Manti in 1878. As senior president of the Salt Lake City 16th Quorum of Seventy, he was unable to meet with his quorum regularly, and this trip allowed him to gather with his brethren and take his position as presiding member.

While those arriving experienced joyful reunions with old friends and family members, many Salt Lake City residents felt the same when family arrived in the city. James E. Talmage, a young educator at the time, commented on the arrival of his parents and brother by saying, "I am thankful that they came."[15]

The E. T. Clark family from Farmington, Utah, used the occasion to host a family reunion, since so many family members planned to be present at the conference and dedication services. "The gathering consisted of nearly one hundred persons all of whom, with one exception, were members of the family," the *Deseret Evening News* reported. Relatives had come from California, Idaho, Wyoming, Arizona, and southern Utah to be in attendance.[16]

For many visitors it had been several years since they had visited the territorial capital. The city, however, had changed not only in size but also in atmosphere. The population of Salt Lake City had been just under thirteen thousand in 1870 and by 1893 was near sixty thousand. Lorenzo Brown, an 1848 Utah pioneer, had moved to Arizona in 1880 from Salt Lake City. On the evening of Brown's arrival he wrote that he found the city "very little like the Salt Lake City of twelve years ago." On the following day he noted again, "The city cannot be described it must be seen and the contrast between now and then."[17] The difference Brown noticed was not only in size, recent construction, and city improvements but also in mood.[18]

Before 1889 the social, religious, and political mood of the city reflected the Mormon majority's values. Civic leaders were largely Latter-day Saints. This changed when two city mayors were elected, George M. Scott and Robert N. Baskin, both non-Mormons. Using illegal voting tactics and taking advantage of a recent legal decision disenfranchising many Saints, the anti-Mormon Liberal Party gained political control of Salt Lake City during the municipal election of 1890. This control had far-reaching effects on the enforcement of laws and municipal ordinances in the city.

For the first time in Salt Lake City's history, the majority was being ruled by a vocal and often hostile minority. While the new Liberal Party municipal government embarked on a wide range of municipal programs to improve services within the city, the community witnessed an increase in lawlessness and a decrease in public safety. Previous to 1890 Salt Lake was relatively free of crime as compared with other cities of similar size, but from the beginning of Liberal rule, an alarming increase in crime made Salt Lake City comparable in that regard to other western cities.

Salt Lake had a large religious community, supporting thirty-two meetinghouses, the Saints having built the most of any other single religious group in the city. The Methodists, however, had five churches, including one African Methodist Episcopal Church. The Baptists, Catholics, Congregationalists, and Presbyterians each had two churches, the Episcopalians and Lutherans had three each, and the Christian Scientists had one building. A Jewish community of over one hundred members also was a part of the religious dimension of the city.

This diverse religious community was apprehensive of the changes they were witnessing and were often critical of the Liberal Party's rule. For example, the Methodist Church in Salt Lake City held an "indignation meeting" on 29 December 1890 to "protest against the vice and wickedness existing in the city."[19]

Local newspapers, in an effort to warn conference visitors who may have been unaware of the rising crime rate in the city, had for several days run stories on the danger of "gangs" and "pickpockets" who were roaming the streets. "Be on the lookout," the *Deseret Evening News* warned in bold headlines on 4 April.[20]

N. W. Clayton lost two thousand dollars worth of personal items, including a valuable diamond pin, when an "infamous gang" entered his residence. A conference visitor staying with the Clayton family also lost a gold watch in the robbery. A few days later the paper ran another story about Mr. Lars Peterson of Hyrum, Utah, who was "among the victims of the crooks now in the city." The story continued:

> Yesterday as he stepped off the train at the Union Pacific depot to board a street car, he felt a mysterious influence at work in one of his pockets. It was only a brief moment. As he turned around in the crowd to see if he could discover any solution of the mystery, it was gone and with it his purse, containing his money and return tickets for himself and family. The repeated warnings to beware of pickpockets are evidently not unfounded.[21]

Even the city's police chief was not immune from these activities. "Soon after midnight this morning [7 April] a burglar entered the premises of Chief of Police Paul on Second South between Fifth and Sixth East streets."[22]

Providentially, the majority of visitors to Salt Lake City moved about unmolested during this joyous occasion. Generally Mormon and non-Mormon citizens were courteous and helpful to the visitors, which made the experience even more enjoyable.

The Church reached out to the non-Mormon community during this period in several ways. On one occasion, just days before conference began, the Church opened the doors of the Tabernacle to Miss Blanche B. Cox of London, England. Miss

Cox, a captain of the Salvation Army, lectured in the Tabernacle on 30 March to a large congregation about the "mission of the Army."[23]

Another group, the Scots of Utah, took advantage of the proceedings by holding their "Caledonian Convention" in the city on 7 April, when many Scots would be in town. The meeting was "held in the Wasatch Hall [and] was well attended." James Moffatt of Salt Lake was elected president; "Dr. J. S. Gordon of Ogden, vice president; [and] John Hutchinson of Ogden, secretary."[24]

Besides family reunions, business meetings, and social gatherings, additional Church meetings were also held in conjunction with conference. The Deseret Sunday School Union held its annual meeting on 7 April. It was a special occasion because the founder of the Church's Sunday School was present.

Assistant general superintendent George Goddard welcomed everyone present. "It was over forty-four years ago when the first Sunday school was organized in this valley by a man who has been faithful ever since," Goddard stated. "He is here and I would like him to stand up . . . so all may see him," he continued.[25] Richard Ballantyne then rose. His little group had grown to include some nine thousand officers and over sixty-seven thousand children.

Contemporary newspapers, diaries, and journals reveal another aspect of the drama of the dedication season. Many faithful Saints died during the period between the capstone-laying services and the dedication. Edward Hunter, Jacob Gates, Charles Lambert, William Kartchner, Lot Smith, Melissa N. Allred, Lucy M. Smith, Susan S. Young, Elizabeth Haven Barlow, and Jens C. A. Weibye were among these faithful Saints who wore out their lives in the service to the restored gospel, who died during the period of preparation for the dedication.

Several other early converts and Utah pioneers died just days and weeks before it was possible to enter the completed temple. Like their fellow Saints, these courageous and dedicated people watched for nearly forty years as the temple rose from its foundation to its lofty state. They contributed labor, offerings, and prayers for its speedy erection. Now just before the joyous celebration,

they slipped from this mortal life, unable to physically walk into the temple at its dedication.

Olive Farr, wife of Winslow Farr and mother of Lorin Farr, died at the age of ninety-two on 12 March, just weeks before the dedication. She converted to the restored gospel in Vermont in 1832, gathered to Kirtland with her family in 1837, and subsequently moved to Missouri, Illinois, and Utah.

Another early convert to the Church, William F. Cahoon, died on 5 April, just a day before the first session of dedication. Cahoon was born in Ohio in 1813 and joined the Church before his twentieth birthday. He was a member of Zion's Camp, was ordained to the office of seventy in the priesthood in 1835, and worked on the Nauvoo Temple before coming to Utah. Such stalwart individuals contributed in many ways to the temple's completion and dreamed of the day when they could enter into its sacred precincts, but it was not to be.

The month of April began on a holiday, Arbor Day. Governor Thomas issued a proclamation that 1 April would be observed as Arbor Day, when all Utah citizens should plant trees.[26] Along with the activities of conference and dedication, the Saints respected the governor's request and took time to beautify their city lots, yards, fields, and communities by planting trees. For others connected with the conference and dedication proceedings, it was a day of work. L. John Nuttall, for instance, "read the proof slips of the Dedicatory prayer of the Temple."[27]

As conference began, Church leaders pled with the Saints to settle their differences and to promote love within their families, communities, church, and business associations. President Woodruff promised the Saints who followed this counsel and repented of their sins that the Lord would forgive them and blot their transgressions out so that they would "not be proclaimed to the assembled world."[28]

J. Golden Kimball told the Saints that "our entering into the now completed Temple in this city with pure hearts and good intentions may be the stepping stone to the enjoyment of an increased portion of the gifts and blessings of God."[29]

Many Saints internalized the message and the call for repentance, as B. H. Roberts confided in his journal: "To me this is the most precious assurance and blessing of them all. Help me oh Father to attain unto it; and I will serve Thee forever. How good and precious are Thy gifts, oh my Father! I will try for this blessing. Do Thou, oh God, blot out my transgressions and make me strong against evil forever more."[30]

On the second day of the conference, President Wilford Woodruff said:

I have a request I wish to make of this assembly of Latter-day Saints. . . . I have a desire in my heart that every one of you, the night before you go into the Temple, before retiring to rest, will go by yourselves, in secret prayer. Offer up your prayers to the Lord, and pray that your sins may not only be forgiven, but that you may all have the Spirit of God and the testimony of the Lord Jesus Christ; that the Spirit of God may be with those who assemble in that Temple.[31]

Church leaders had for some time promised great spiritual blessings as a result of the temple's dedication. In 1871, George Q. Cannon had testified:

I fully believe that when that temple is once finished there will be a power and manifestations of the goodness of God unto this people such as they have never before experienced. Every work of this kind that we have accomplished has been attended with increased and wonderful results unto us as a people—an increase of power and of God's blessings upon us. It was so in Kirtland and at Nauvoo; at both places the Elders had an increase of power, and the Saints, since the completion of, and the administration of ordinances in, those buildings have had a power they never possessed previously.[32]

With the promises clearly before them, the Saints finished their spiritual preparations along with the physical preparations.

The Paris art missionaries prepared murals for this room to depict a garden motif.

63

The finishing touches on the temple interior were completed on the afternoon of 5 April. In the evening, general Church officers escorted non-Mormon government officials and prominent businessmen and wives through the temple on a first-of-its-kind tour.

This experience gave the non-Latter-day Saint community an opportunity to visit the temple before it was closed to the general public. "In fact," as a contemporary reflection noted, "members of the Church cannot [following the dedication services] enter the building for the gratification of curiosity alone. If they go there it must be for the purpose of attending to ordinances."[33]

A large number of nonmembers of the Church and former opponents from the community, and some from the East, visited the temple during the open house by invitation of the First Presidency. For some Saints, this new policy of allowing non-Latter-day Saints to walk through the temple just before the dedication services was unexpected. Joseph Henry Dean noted in his journal: "At 5 p.m. the Governor, Judges, lawyers, and [principal] outsiders were permitted to enter and [were] shown all through the building. This was a great surprise to me and most everyone else I suppose." In a final reflection, he explained, "It won't hurt the temple and will allay a great deal of prejudice."[34]

Many nonmembers of the Church who visited the temple were thoroughly impressed by the workmanship evident in the building and by the kindness shown them by Church leaders. Describing his visit to the temple during the open house (and making particular note of the mural paintings), a reporter from a local newspaper enthusiastically wrote:

It is upon the first floor that the magnificence and splendor of the decorations and furnishings burst upon the spectator, who passes in wonder and amazement from one scene of beauty to visions still more enchanting. . . . In [the Garden Room] the genius of the artist has transferred vividly realistic scenes to the walls and ceilings. Forest scenery, streams, mountains and wild beasts are depicted with such marvelous skill . . . that the spectator is almost convinced that he is standing in the midst of the creation wilds.[35]

The *Salt Lake Tribune,* in a period of transition towards a more friendly attitude about the Church, published a surprisingly positive article about the temple dedication in its morning edition on 6 April 1893. The headline read, "A genuine surprise on the city yesterday afternoon. People to the number of about 5,000, mostly gentiles, visited the temple yesterday evening by special invitations issued by the Mormon Church Authorities."[36]

The *Tribune* said that many people who knew the temple would be closed to them following the dedication rushed "to take advantage of the privilege if possible." The tour was very much appreciated and enjoyed by those who visited the building. "The interior [of the temple] was a revelation of beauty" the article stated, "from the first to the last apartment."[37]

H. R. Harper, editor of the Chattanooga, Tennessee *News,* arrived in Salt Lake City to spend two days in the city, but he was so delighted with the "picturesque surroundings of the city and the cordial hospitality of the people" that he stayed longer. "I considered it a great privilege to be permitted yesterday to inspect the great Temple and feel amply repaid for my long journey."[38]

Mr. Harper reported, "In leaving Salt Lake City and Utah I shall carry away with me pleasant memories of the Saints as an honest, industrious and God-fearing people, who have done great things for the amelioration of mankind and who have made a desert to blossom like a rose."[39] Joseph Dean was right; the pre-dedication tour helped build a new bridge between the Saints and their neighbors.

While many former opponents of the Church visited the holy edifice by invitation of President Woodruff, Church women met in the Relief Society conference held at the Social Hall.

The *Deseret Evening News* published several articles in its issues of 5-6 April 1893 about the temple, including a history and description of the temple design. The Church decided to print these articles as a souvenir publication in the form of a pamphlet entitled *House of the Lord: Historical and Descriptive Sketch of the Salt Lake Temple* "for the convenience and information of visitors to the Temple and others at a distance." The newspaper announced:

> In order to make the pamphlet still more complete and worthy of being considered a souvenir of the occasion, the full text of the Dedicatory Prayer will be appended. Numerous illustrations will adorn the booklet, which will number about 40 pages. It will be ready after the close of the morning services in the Temple tomorrow [6 April 1893], and may be purchased at the *Deseret News* and the *Juvenile Instructor* offices.[40]

The final preparation of the dedication ceremonies occurred when the Church convened in general conference beginning on Tuesday, 4 April 1893. During the two days of conference, Church leaders taught the Saints about the temple dedication and the preparations necessary to enter into such a sacred and holy place.

"President Wilford Woodruff presided," a local paper noted, "which fact was very gratifying to all who attended."[41] His instruction was most appreciated by the Saints who gathered from all over the United States, Mexico, and Canada. His remarks were "very comforting, his kindly counsel and tender manner of expressing himself working a deep and lasting impression upon all those who sat within the sound of his voice."[42] President Woodruff himself felt good about the conference as he wrote in his journal at the close of the day, "The power of God was with us."[43]

For many Saints, especially those from distant locations, the time in Salt Lake City allowed them to visit both old and new Church buildings. "After being absent from Salt Lake so many years," Lucy Flake wrote, "it is grand to again listen to the great organ and feel the inspiration by being in those sacred buildings." She concluded, "It brings tears of joy to my eyes."[44]

The numbers of Saints arriving in Salt Lake City surprised Church leaders. It quickly became evident that the scheduled dedication services would not accommodate the growing numbers of visitors. L. John Nuttall noted that a special meeting was held on the first day of conference with stake priesthood leaders to discuss the situation. "Attended meeting of Presidents of Stakes," Nuttall recorded, "to arrange for admission of additional members from their stakes to the Temple dedication."[45] The result of the meeting was announced in the *Deseret Evening News*:

> AN EXTRA SESSION. An extra session of the temple dedication services will be held on Friday evening, April 7th. Doors will open at 5:30 p.m. Admission for this session will be at the East Gate only. The following apportionment has been made for this special session. Mexico, 15; Star Valley, 40; San Luis, 50; St. Joseph, 20; St. Johns, 25; Maricopa, 38; Bannock, 100; San Juan, 25; St. George, 25; Panguitch, 50 ; Parowan, 50; Emery, 35; Beaver, 60; Malad, 25; Kanab, 30; Bear Lake, 150; Utah, 700; and Choir (Sanpete), 50.[46]

All things were now ready for the historic dedication services.

President Wilford Woodruff on 6 April 1893.

9

"The Spirit of God Filled the House"

The culmination of forty years of Latter-day Saint effort and sacrifice ended when President Wilford Woodruff entered the temple on the last day of the Church's annual conference, 6 April 1893, to dedicate the edifice. President Woodruff led the congregation into the temple through the southwest doors in the morning for the first dedication service that began at ten o'clock in the morning.

Many witnesses of the dedicatory services left records of the proceedings, including the official minutes. Susa Young Gates was called as the official stenographer for the temple dedication services, and she faithfully recorded the events of the day.

One contemporary journal entry describes the weather on 6 April as "cold [and] dusty." A strong breeze from the northwest gradually increased until about ten o'clock, when it became a "blowing gale."[1] A local newspaper reported a "wind velocity of sixty miles per hour. This is the highest velocity ever recorded at the Salt Lake [weather] station."[2]

"It had been predicted [that] the Devil would howl," one participant noted, "and sure enough he did, for Salt Lake City had never witnessed such a storm, wind, rain and snow, many houses and trees were blown over. . . . Hundreds of people stood in the snow for hours waiting for the temple doors to open."[3] The storm lasted until the dedication service was over, subsiding as the Saints began to file out of the temple. The weather also turned much colder. Joseph Dean recorded, "The temperature must have fallen into the two or three hours fully 25 degrees."[4]

George Edward Anderson, a Utah photographer bent on capturing the event through his camera, had set up a portable photographic gallery for the dedication services to induce visitors to have their photographs taken on the historic occasion. The tent gallery suffered the effects of the windstorm and was smashed, which made it impossible to proceed with his work. A sign, "No Pictures Taken Today," was placed in front of the tent. While Anderson attempted to fix his tent gallery, those wishing to participate in the services began to line up outside the temple gates in the bad weather in preparation for the services.

Waiting for entrance into the first session of the temple dedication was a difficult ordeal for some of the old and feeble members because of the weather conditions. "In going up the temple stairs to the morning services of the first day," Benjamin Johnson reported, "and feeling the weight of my overcoat, I left it by the way."[5] Johnson regretted having left his coat at the entrance of the temple because at the end of the first session the participants were ushered out the opposite stairway. "I came without my coat to meet the blasts of a raging storm or tornado. . . . The air soon became full of snow and the cold was intense." He required nearly two hours to return to the entrance where he had laid his coat earlier because of the "stream of people crowding in as the afternoon congregation" was already lining up for admittance.[6]

The Temple Block gates opened at eight-thirty, and the street was packed long before that hour. Two hours were required to admit "one by one the 2,200 people," a temple assistant noted.[7]

Thomas Griggs, a member of the Tabernacle

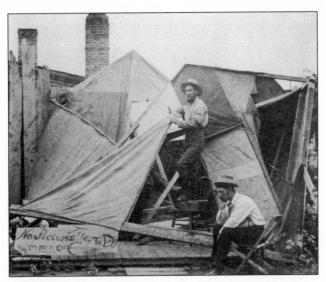

George Edward Anderson's temporary tent gallery was blown down on the first day of the dedication services.

Choir, arrived at the south gate at 8:20 A.M., but the line was so long that "it was 9:55 a.m. when I was ten feet from the [gate]," he wrote.

> Wind, dust, and little rain had come and it was very uncomfortable, to be ended by the door keeper to the remainder announcing "no more can be admitted come tomorrow evening." Getting desperate I pushed forward and being well known as a soloist of the choir got into the yard and was taken to the south west entrance and hurriedly passed through the rooms, some magnificent. Crowding along the jam and reached Bro. E. Stephens who passed me a [choir] book . . . and directed me to be sent into the gathering. The 300 voice choir then sang . . . with good effect.[8]

Heber Bennion arrived in the city after a one-hour drive "to be on time for the dedicatory services of the Temple." He stood in the long line with his "fellow Bishopric" members for two hours "on the street . . . midst wind, dust and noises," but was unable to enter when the building became filled.[9]

Those unable to attend the first two sessions were invited to a meeting held in the Tabernacle nearby. Numerous speakers spoke on a wide range of subjects, including the history of the construc-tion of the Salt Lake Temple. Those in the congregation were allowed to "bear their testimonies" about God's work in the open meeting. At the same time, several thousand Saints met in the upper assembly room of the temple to participate in one of the many dedicatory sessions.

On several occasions, remarks were made regarding those who had been at the laying of the cornerstones some forty years earlier. Only a few of the General Authorities present then were in attendance at the dedication services. While reflecting upon former friends and Church leaders who had gone before, Church leaders nevertheless focused on the new generation present. While the temple was under construction, "a new generation [had] grown up, and upon them," George Q. Cannon stated, "the labors rest of carrying forward the work of God."[10] Those responsibilities rested not only on those present but also on the great number of Church members not present, whether in Utah or in some distant land.

The "hopes, desires, and anticipations of the entire Church have been centered upon the completion of this edifice in the principal city of Zion," Church leaders noted earlier. They reminded the Saints that the "eyes of the members of the Church in every land have been lovingly directed toward it."[11] In fact, B. H. Roberts noted, "Some of the distant Stakes of Zion . . . had paid toward the erection of the Temple double the portion that had been allotted to them."[12] Now the day had arrived to celebrate the completion of this great project.

The first day witnessed two dedication services, both held in the fourth floor assembly hall of the newly completed temple. A contemporary newspaper account described this assembly room in its 7 April issue:

> The [fourth] floor is wholly taken up by the Grand Assembly room. It has a seating capacity of 2,200 and is 120x80 feet and 36 feet high. . . . This room is also decorated in white and gold, and is of surpassing beauty and grandeur. The lofty elliptical ceilings, artistically panelled, is studded with 300 incandescent lights, which, with the fine large electroliers, fill the room with dazzling radiance. A

graceful gallery, with light bronze railing, sweeps around the entire room. It is reached by circular stairways at each of the four corners.

At each end of the room there are pulpits for the church authorities, arranged in tiers . . . upholstered in crimson plush. The Melchizedek priesthood occupies the east tiers and the Aaronic those on the west. The seats are of pure white, upholstered in crimson, and are reversible, so that the audience may face either pulpit. There are also a large number of opera chairs, upholstered in plush.[13]

All the members of the First Presidency and the Quorum of the Twelve Apostles were present—except Moses Thatcher who was ill—with their wives and some family members. The wives of deceased Apostles were also present along with a number of general and local Church priesthood leaders (stake presidencies, bishops, and Relief Society presidencies). The spacious hall was filled to its capacity, as many as twenty-two hundred individuals.

John D. T. McAllister recorded his observations regarding the first day's session in his journal:

Attended the dedicatory services, Salt Lake Temple. President Wilford Woodruff presiding. Presidents George Q. Cannon and Joseph F. Smith and the [Council] of the Twelve, except Brother Moses Thatcher, sick, and the First Seven Presidents of Seventies, Presidents of Stakes and Counselors, and all Presiding authorities who were in the city were present. Three hundred members of the Tabernacle Choir, under the directions of Elder Evan Stephens [sang] the Anthem, "Let Israel Join and Sing."[14]

A large pipe organ had been set up in the assembly room to accompany the choir during the services. The three-hundred-voice choir sang hymns written exclusively by LDS composers, several of which were especially written for the occasion. The women of the choir were dressed in white and the men in dark suits. Annie Wells Cannon wrote, "During the temple dedication the people of Utah had a wonderful and beautiful revelation concerning the divine art [of music]." She continued:

Did any of us really know before the talent of our musicians? From the morning of the first meeting, when the three hundred trained voices, under the baton of our admired Evan Stephens, pealed forth those beautiful anthems and hymns until the close of the three weeks during which not only the Salt Lake Choir but also the choirs of Utah, Weber, Cache and Sanpete Counties sang for us there was a continual and delightful surprise. . . . Surely all who listened to the divine and inspiring strains during the conference will no longer doubt their ability to compose and will bestow just praise on all. The words alone, so appropriate and sweet, the music tender yet sublime and the most perfect rendition made a feast for the soul.[15]

Charles R. Savage also recorded his reflections on the divine influence he felt as a member of the choir during the services:

Sang with the Choir in the first dedication ceremony in the Temple. Never in my life did I feel an influence like unto the one I felt during the ceremony—every heart was touched with the divinity of our surroundings. I never felt a better influence in my life. I never had more great joy than I felt—my soul was filled with peace and my whole nature replete with satisfaction. The ceremony lasted four hours. The talks were inspiring. The music rendered by 300 members of the Choir was all original and very fine. I never felt nearer to the invisible powers than while in the Temple. I never had a stronger testimony than on this occasion.[16]

Another member of the choir, Bardella S. Curtis, not only felt a heavenly spirit during the service but also saw "the veil between mortality and high heaven drawn aside." She was permitted to "see some of the things beyond," including significant events in the past, like Joseph Smith's First Vision in 1820.[17]

A temple dedication pass for admittance to the afternoon session on 6 April 1893.

The service included the dedicatory prayer offered by President Woodruff, talks by all three members of the Church's First Presidency, and the rendering of the awe-inspiring sacred Hosanna Shout, led by Lorenzo Snow with "the entire audience standing upon their feet and waving white handkerchiefs in concert," Francis Hammond wrote.[18] For Brother Hammond, "it seemed the heavenly host had come down to mingle with us."[19] Emmeline B. Wells noted: "This shout of Hosanna thrilled the hearts of the vast multitude, and echoed grandly through the magnificent building; so exultant and enraptured were the saints in their rejoicing that their faces beamed with gladness, and the whole place seemed glorified and sanctified in recognition of the consecration made on that momentous and never-to-be-forgotten occasion."[20]

L. John Nuttall wrote that the shout was "rendered with a hearty good will, my heart and soul," he continued, "were so full of the spirit of the Lord, that I could scarcely contain myself."[21] At the conclusion of the soul-stirring shout, the choir immediately began singing a specially composed hymn. Choir member Thomas Griggs wrote, "Choir sang Brother Evan Stephen's 'Hosannah Chorus,' the congregation joining in the latter part with the 'Spirit of God Like a Fire Is Burning.'"[22]

The Spirit of God like a fire is burning!
The latter-day glory begins to come forth;
The visions and blessings of old are returning,
And angels are coming to visit the earth.

We'll sing and we'll shout with
    the armies of heaven,
Hosanna, hosanna to God and the Lamb!
Let glory to them in the highest be given,
Henceforth and forever, Amen and amen!

The combined effect of some twenty-five hundred people standing together in the upper assembly room of the temple, all joining together in the sacred shout and singing the dedication hymn, was overpowering. Many participants wept uncontrollably; others could not finish the hymn as they were so overcome by the spirit of the occasion.

While the shout and the combined choir and congregational singing was a never-to-be-forgotten experience, the focus of the ceremony was the dedicatory prayer offered by President Wilford Woodruff. After "making a few explanatory remarks and then kneeling on a plush, covered stool provided for the purpose, he offered the dedicatory prayer—reading it."[23]

Brigham Young Academy student Amy Brown, later Relief Society general president, went to the temple with her future father-in-law, Francis M. Lyman. She recalled: "It was one of the most thrilling spiritual experiences of my life. . . . [President Woodruff] stood there before the people with hair and beard as white as snow, the essence of purity, gentleness, and faithfulness, he reminded me of the prophets of old."[24]

The prayer began as follows:

Our Father in heaven, thou who hast created the heavens and the earth, and all things that are therein; thou most glorious One, perfect in mercy, love, and truth, we, thy children, come this day before thee, and in this house which we have built to thy most holy name, humbly plead the atoning blood of thine Only Begotten Son, that our sins may be remembered no more against us forever, but that our prayers may ascend unto thee and have free access to thy throne, that we may be heard in thy holy habitation. And may it graciously please thee to hearken unto our petitions, answer them according to thine infinite wisdom and love, and grant that the blessings which we seek may be bestowed upon us, even a hundred fold, inasmuch as we seek with purity of heart and fullness of purpose to do thy will and glorify thy name.[25]

In this inspired prayer, President Woodruff asked the Lord to bless the Saints and to accept "this building in all its parts from foundation to capstone" that it might be "an abode of thy well-beloved Son, our Savior." President Woodruff asked the Lord to remember "all those who have labored in the erection of this house, or who have, in any way, by their means or influence aided in its completion." He prayed that the Lord's blessing would be with all Church officers and missionaries. He pled for the Jews, "thy stricken people of the House of Judah. Oh, deliver them from those that oppress them." He asked the Lord to remember the people of Lehi, the native Indians of North and South America.[26]

President Woodruff thanked the Lord for the "patriotic men" who laid the foundation of the United States government. He asked the Lord to bless the "President, his Cabinet, and Congress." President Woodruff's supplication reached beyond the Church and the United States as he asked the Lord to bless the leaders of all governments and people everywhere. He concluded by saying:

And now, our Father, we bless thee, we praise thee, we glorify thee, we worship thee, day by day we magnify thee and give thee thanks for thy great goodness towards us, thy children, and we pray thee, in the name of thy Son, Jesus Christ, our Savior, to hear these our humble petitions, and answer us from heaven, thy holy dwelling place, where thou sittest enthroned in glory, might, majesty and dominion, and with an infinitude of power which we, thy mortal creatures, cannot imagine, much less comprehend. Amen and amen.[27]

The prayer was "not only impressive, but comprehensive," wrote stake president Rudger Clawson. It covered "a wide range of subjects outside of the temple."[28] According to John Henry Smith, the prayer "took thirty-five minutes" to read.[29] Francis M. Lyman noted, "He read it unhesitatingly without glasses."[30]

Not only had President Woodruff read unhesitatingly, he spoke clearly and with power during the reading so that he could be heard plainly in the large assembly hall. "He offered the prayer seemingly with [the] strength of a man fifty years old," one participant wrote.[31] President Woodruff was eighty-six years of age at the time.

For President Woodruff, this occasion was the fulfillment of a dream he had several years earlier. He confided in his journal: "Near[ly] fifty years ago while in the city of Boston I had a vision of going with the Saints to the Rocky Mountains building a temple and I dedicated it. Two nights in succession before John Taylor's death [1887] President Brigham Young [who had died ten years earlier] gave me the keys of the temple and told me to go and dedicate it, which I did."[32]

Contemporary journals and diaries used various words and phrases to describe the experience. Andrew Jenson said the meeting was full of "emotion and power," which "deeply stirred" his soul and indicated that the "Spirit of God filled the house."[33] L. John Nuttall indicated that the talks given by Church leaders were not only powerful, but were given "very feelingly," and as a result he "never felt so well in my life. I cannot express my feelings."[34]

James Bunting said, "It would be in vain for me to attempt a description of the interior of the Temple or to describe the heavenly feeling that pervaded all the exercises."[35] One account simply stated, "Each must see and hear and feel for himself."[36]

President Woodruff later told a congregation of Saints that "the Heavenly Host were in attendance at the [first] dedication [service] . . . and if the eyes of the congregation could be opened they would [have] seen Joseph and Hyrum [Smith], Brigham Young, John Taylor and all the good men who had lived in this dispensation assembled with us, as also Esaias, Jeremiah, and all the Holy Prophets and Apostles who had prophesied of the latter day work." President Woodruff continued, "They were rejoicing with us in this building which had been accepted of the Lord and [when] the [Hosanna] shout had reached the throne of the Almighty," they too had joined in the joyous shout.[37]

Rudger Clawson journal entry for 6 April 1893. Note the newspaper clipping describing the features of the completed temple.

During his remarks to the congregation, President Woodruff prophesied "that there would be a change and the Saints would see things they never dreamt of."[38] This prophecy received considerable attention in the non-Mormon press. The *Los Angeles Times,* for example, stated: "President Woodruff . . . uttered a prophecy concerning the future of the people of God. The prophecy was not divulged, but it is understood to refer to the growth of the prosperity of the church and the increased happiness of the Saints."[39]

Joseph F. Smith followed President Woodruff and "expressed his feelings and commended the brethren who had been foremost in aiding to complete the building in [the] time appointed."[40]

Family members of General Authorities were present at this first session of dedication. For ex-

ample, Joseph Fielding Smith, son of President Joseph F. Smith and later a Church president, attended. As "a young man holding the Aaronic Priesthood, it was my privilege," he recalled, "to be present at the opening session. With others holding the Aaronic Priesthood I had a place in the gallery on the north side of the assembly room. I was greatly impressed with the wonderful spirit of these exercises and have looked back to that day many times with deep feelings of satisfaction."[41]

Following the dedication service on 6 April 1893, President Woodruff noted in his personal journal: "The spirit and power of God rested upon us. The spirit of prophecy and revelation was upon us and the hearts of the people were melted and many things were unfolded to us."[42]

San Francisco Chronicle.

VOL. LVII. SAN FRANCISCO, CAL., FRIDAY, APRIL 7, 1893. NO. 82.

THE HOUSE OF MORMON

Saints Dedicate Their Big Temple.

Curious Ceremonies Held in Secret.

The Work of Forty Years Crowned by a Great Festival—Sketch of the Building.

THE MORMON TEMPLE.

TABERNACLE, SALT LAKE CITY.

BIG CRUISERS AT DRILL

Evolutions of Our Marine Cavalry.

Getting Into Trim for the Review.

White-Hulled Ships-of-War Move in Line and Column by Endless Signals.

PERU MUST EXPLAIN.

Outrage on an American Consul.

Police Watched a Mob at Work.

The Building Sacked and the Officer in Charge Shot in the Foot.

HEMP IN THEIR HANDS

LYNCHERS ABOUND A KANSAS JAIL.

A Woman and Her Little Daughter Terribly Maltreated at Salina.

San Francisco Chronicle edition of 7 April 1893. Proceedings of the dedication services were published in many non-Mormon newspapers throughout the nation.

Heber Bennion braved that day's windstorm and returned home to find his barn and sheds blown down. He wrote, "The Temple stood the storm as an offering went up before the Lord, while the barn tumbled."[43] Bennion saw these events as being spiritually symbolic: the work of men—represented by Bennion's barn and sheds—must fall; but the work of God—represented by the temple—will stand forever.

On the night of the first dedication services, 6 April, a special musical program called the "National Children's Concert" was held in the Tabernacle for conference visitors. Some "1,200 took part, it was very inspiring."[44] Many children were dressed in their "characteristic costume" for the occasion.[45] Annie Wells Cannon wrote:

The concerts in the large tabernacle afforded much pleasure to our visitors as well as ourselves. Being a people gathered from all parts of the world it is very delightful to listen now and then to the national songs of our native lands, especially when so enthusiastically sung by our little ones. Our own dear song, "The Star-spangled Banner," is always new, though we heard it every hour and the heart beats a response to every word like a martial accompaniment.[46]

A young "beautiful Mexican" child draped in white "posed up on a niche in the great organ" some forty feet above the audience. One four-year-old boy, however, Master Pedersen, was "the great attraction of the evening." He "performed on the violin [and] executed many pieces in a masterly style, his father accompanied him on the piano," Francis Hammond noted.[47]

Jane Blood reflected on the event: "It was lovely, nothing pleases me so much as the little children. I could spend all my time with them." Following the concert Jane returned home to Bountiful on the midnight train.[48]

Finally, the first day of dedication services was completed. Similar services were held on successive days through 18 April and again on 23-24 April. Two sessions were held most days, except on 7 April when an evening session was added to accommodate the large crowds who came to partici-

pate in the dedication of the Salt Lake Temple. The *Deseret News Weekly* stated, "It is a thoroughly conservative calculation to say that the dedication services have been attended by 75,000 people."[49] While a great spirit was manifested during the first day of the services, similar feelings and observations about the dedication occurred in the successive meetings. For many, however, the two-hour services "were altogether too short."[50]

Joseph Dean, a temple assistant, noted in his journal on 10 April: "The service today was the best of any day yet. Every meeting seems to me to be more inspiring than the preceding one."[51]

San Francisco, California, residents picked up their daily newspaper, the *San Francisco Chronicle*, on 7 April to discover a front-page headline article entitled, "The House of Mormon: The Saints Dedicate Their Big Temple." The full three-column article included a large illustration of the "Mormon Temple" in Salt Lake City. The reporter described the interior as "gorgeously furnished and adorned." The "interior decorations," he further stated, "consisting of massive moldings, ornamental figures and beautiful paintings, cost vast sums of money."[52]

The Associated Press news service, which had reporters in attendance at the open house the day before the dedication, carried the dedication story over its wire service; as a result, newspapers from the *New York Times* on the East Coast to the *Los Angeles Times* on the West Coast printed the historic events in Salt Lake City in their papers.[53] The Los Angeles newspaper headlines, written in large, bold print, stated, "Happy Saints." The subheading continued, "The Dedication of the Great Mormon Temple. The Barren Spot That 'Tithes' Have Caused to Bloom. Sixty-third Anniversary of the Church of Latter Day Saints. The Architecture of the Building Without a Known Parallel—Yesterday's Services and the Dedication Ceremonies. By Telegraph to *The Times*."[54]

The *Constitution-Democrat* reported in bold headlines, "Mormons Rejoice." The article, which was very favorable—even laudatory—about the Saints' efforts to complete and dedicate the "magnificent Temple," reported that Saints from "Canada to Mexico, from Europe to the islands of the Pacific [had] journeyed to" Salt Lake City to witness the event.[55]

In most cases, the story was the lead article on 7 April 1893, and while most praised the Saints for their efforts, some were skeptical that the temple would remain a monument of Latter-day Saint faith.

A Pittsburgh, Pennsylvania, newspaper predicted, "The evident fact is that Mormonism, wounded as it is, must eventually die, and someone now living may yet see the great building dedicated April 6 occupied as a Methodist, Episcopal or Presbyterian Western University."[56] While reporters throughout the United States made the dedication of the temple on 6 April a major news story, the Saints looked forward to more eventful days ahead.

Three sessions—morning, afternoon, and evening—were held on Friday, 7 April. George F. Richards, his wife, Alice, his sister-in-law Estella, and the two oldest Richards children, George and Alice Minerva, went to the fourth session.[57] Alice Minerva recalled, "Papa and Mama took me to the dedication of the Salt Lake Temple. I still thrill when I think of what I saw and heard."[58]

Alice Minerva Richards was baptized and confirmed—also receiving at this time, as is standard in the Church, the gift of the Holy Ghost—on 3 April 1893, just a few days before her visit to the temple. While in the Salt Lake Temple, an outpouring of the Spirit came in a way never forgotten by the young eight-year-old girl: "I witnessed a 'Heavenly Manifestation' at the time of the dedication of the Temple and heard beautiful music, beyond anything I have heard elsewhere. I was only eight years old and saw angels on the ceiling. I have always been grateful for the privilege of attending on that sacred occasion."[59] Alice Minerva excitedly returned home and told her younger brothers and sister about the experience she witnessed in the sacred building.

During the same meeting, Thomas Sleight noted that the entire congregation assembled "joined in mentally with [Joseph F. Smith who read the prayer] making their humble offering and petition to the Great Elohiem in the name of Jesus Christ."[60] For Thomas, the effect of the prayer was overwhelming, "For I felt," he wrote, "that I stood in the presence of God and a feeling of reverence came over me that I never experienced be-

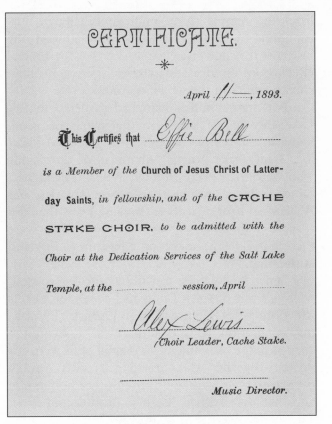

A Cache Stake Choir certificate for admittance to temple dedication services.

fore." The effect was such that "love and charity" overcame him, and for the first time he understood Jesus' words on the cross, "Father, forgive them; for they know not what they do."[61]

The meeting finally ended, but for Thomas Sleight and his wife, "to leave the temple was like coming down from heaven to earth and if I did not know it was the will of the Lord, I should have looked at the task with sadness." He confided in his diary that he prayed that "the heavenly feeling might not entirely leave me" during the coming days.[62]

The special evening session held on 7 April was well attended. James Bunting wrote, "I had the privilege of going through the Temple again on Thursday evening and attending the services by the light of electricity which [effect] was most sublime."[63] The *Chicago Tribune* reported the temple was "ablaze with splendor" at night. The article continued: "The hundreds of windows threw gleams of light far into the outer darkness, while from the temple spires high above all the surrounding buildings the lights shot athwart the heavens. It is universally conceded that for general effect, both interior and exterior, there is no finer church edifice in the whole of America."[64]

For many families who had gathered in Salt Lake City to participate in the joyous occasion, being in the temple together was an added blessing. Lucy Flake noted: "Members of our family who were there were Mother, William, Prudence, James and Joel, my brothers Orson, Charles, and William and parts of their families. I was thankful that we could all go together. All my brothers were there but Hyrum, he was on a mission to England at the time."[65]

James E. Talmage had tickets for one session, while his out-of-town family had admission tickets for another day. He noted in his journal: "By making application to the authorities, I secured a change in the assignment, so that all of us were admitted together this morning. I was doubly pleased to walk with and through that holy house and that with Father, Mother, Brother and Wife. The services were most impressive."[66]

Widows and orphans were not forgotten during this special season of rejoicing. Personal invitations for the family members of deceased Church leaders were sent, and their family members were made welcome. Whether Truman O. Angell's wife, Susan, attended the dedication is uncertain. She died on 18 July 1893, just three months following the first service. Wilford Woodruff's personal secretary went to "the temple services [on 11 April] with the late William W. Taylor's four . . . and got them good seats" before he went back to his own office to work.[67]

Church leaders met between meetings in their new offices in the temple. On 16 April, the Council of the Twelve met for the first formal meeting in the Apostles' room at six o'clock in the evening, following two sessions of dedication. President Lorenzo Snow dedicated the room and led the group in prayer for Moses Thatcher, a member of the Twelve who went home to Logan quite ill.[68]

No dedication service was held on Wednesday, 19 April, in the temple. Instead, a special priesthood leadership session convened at 10:00 A.M. with one hundred and ten participants. President Woodruff asked all those present to relate their feelings about the dedication and the services. "All had an opportunity to express themselves, occupying from 2 to 5 minutes each." When all had concluded their remarks, President Woodruff bore a powerful testimony. Among those things recorded in the shorthand report, he said:

I will promise this assembly that the Holy Ghost will bear witness to [you] of the truth of what I say, and it is this, The God of heaven and the Lord Jesus Christ and the heavenly host—I say this to you in the name of Jesus Christ, the Son of God—have accepted the dedication of this Temple at our hands. The God of heaven has accepted this people, has accepted the labor of the Latter-day Saints upon this Temple and accepted the people who have assembled here. The God of heaven has forgiven the sins of the Latter-day Saints [and] those that bear the Priesthood in this room, and those who have been humble before the Lord and have attended this Conference. Their sins are remitted, and will be remitted by the power of God and will not be remembered any more, unless we sin further. And again I say to you that the God of heaven and the heavenly host accept of your offering.[69]

The meeting continued until 6:30 P.M. with a one-and-a-half-hour break. B. H. Roberts summarized well the feelings of those attending: "There was a very heavenly spirit throughout and everyone was melted to tears in the presence of these testimonies."[70] The meeting lasted seven hours, and, according to Elder Marriner Merrill, all had a "glorious time and all felt well."[71]

On the following day, 20 April, First Presidency members George Q. Cannon and Joseph F. Smith "were deeply affected and moved to tears" during their talks to some one hundred and fifteen Church leaders. The service was a fast and testimony meeting, like the one on the day before. All the stakes of the Church except one, including those in Canada and Mexico, were represented in this meeting.

President Cannon's remarks included his personal testimony of the reality of Christ. He said that he "had seen and conversed with [him] as a man talks with his friend." The "feelings of all were subdued" by this powerful apostolic witness.[72] The meeting moved from the Presidency room to the celestial room, where the brethren participated in a special prayer. "President Joseph F. Smith offered up a few words of prayer, after which the brethren prayed . . . , President George Q. Cannon being mouth."[73] At the conclusion of the prayer, this part of the meeting closed when all sang "Praise God from Whom All Blessings Flow." The brethren then went back upstairs to the Presidency room.

Presiding Bishop William B. Preston "blessed and break the bread which was handed to each. . . . Bishop Robert T. Burton, Counselor in the Presiding Bishopric, blessed the wine, and it was placed upon the tables and all partook of the Sacrament."[74] B. H. Roberts noted:

Thus was the Lord's supper truly the sacrament and we ate and drank in memory of *Him*—our Savior and Redeemer, our Advocate with the Father. Every face beamed with happiness and shone with intelligence. After supper we sang a hymn, conversed at pleasure and told our duties and told anecdotes principally of the Prophet Joseph. One could have sat I know not how long but as all things seem to have an end in this world, so did this our meeting.[75]

For another priesthood leader assembled, "it seemed as [though] the Savior was present administering to us in person. I can never forget that supper of the Lord."[76]

From left to right: 1) Wooden mallet that may have been used during the temple capstone services (1892). 2) One of the eight light bulbs that ringed the copper finials capping each spire, used to illuminate the upper structure of the temple. 3) Silver sacrament chalice inscribed with "Holiness to the Lord," used during the special priesthood meeting on 20 April 1893.

Following the administration of the sacrament, those attending listened to stories of early Church history as told by eyewitnesses to the events. Of those present, thirty had been present at the laying of the cornerstones of the temple in 1853; twenty-seven brethren knew the Prophet Joseph Smith; eight had "eaten with the Prophet at his table"; six attended meetings with Joseph Smith in the Kirtland Temple; and one was baptized by the Prophet.

A. O. Smoot and Lorin Farr, among the "eyewitnesses," related personal experiences with Joseph during the early period of Church history. "This was one of the most memorable events of my life," Rudger Clawson recalled. "[The event was an] occasion," he concluded, "never to be forgotten and not easily described."[77]

In the absence of President Woodruff, who left the priesthood meeting the day before very sick, his counselors in the First Presidency concluded the meeting. Joseph F. Smith arose and blessed those present: "May peace be unto you, may the Holy Ghost never forsake you, may you be true and faithful; and come up on the morning of the first resurrection with your wives, and yours."[78] George Q. Cannon followed: "God will help you. . . . You can do anything that God requires of you. . . . There is nothing that comes into your hearts that will be good for Zion, but God will enable you to do. . . . I bless you all. I bless each of you and yours. I seal it upon you by the authority I hold in the name of Jesus Christ Amen."[79]

A closing prayer was offered by Church Patriarch John Smith at 5:45 P.M. L. John Nuttall wrote, "I never enjoyed myself any better in such meetings and felt very grateful that I had been permitted to be one of the one hundred and fifteen brethren present."[80]

Among the stories related by the participants of the temple dedication to their families and friends upon their return home, the special priesthood session was of particular interest. At Kanab, Utah, a brother reported President Woolley's comments:

Friday 28th [April 1893]. President E. D. Woolley having returned from Salt Lake City called a meeting at the Tithing Office and gave an account of a meeting held in the Temple on the 19th and 20th at which there [were] about 115 of the presiding priesthood of the Church. The sacrament was administered after the pattern of the Savior administering it to the Nephites. The spirit of the Lord was manifest in rich effusion and much valuable instruction given. Several of the brethren were called upon to speak who had visited the Conference.[81]

Another special session held during the dedication services was scheduled for Sunday School children under eight years of age. Alice Richards returned home to help her young unbaptized children prepare for their special trip to Salt Lake City. Her husband, George, noted in his diary on Saturday, 22 April: "Alice took the four small children, LeGrand, Joel, Sarah, and Amy to Salt Lake with the Sunday School to see and attend the Temple dedication. I took them to the depot."[82]

LeGrand Richards, age seven at the time and later a member of the Quorum of the Twelve Apostles, attended the special dedication session with his mother, brother, and two sisters. Alice told them that the General Authorities would be there, including their Apostle-grandfather, Franklin D. Richards. She also told them that they would feel a special spirit at the dedication. LeGrand's older sister Alice Minerva related her own experience, which only heightened LeGrand's expectations.

Following the close of the session, Alice took LeGrand, Joel, Sarah, and Amy to greet their aging grandfather as he came down the stand in the assembly room. Later, LeGrand said this was the "first and only time" he remembered meeting his grandfather. He was impressed with all the Church leaders, especially Wilford Woodruff; LeGrand said that for the rest of his life he recalled exactly what the Church President looked like and his dress. During an oral history interview, LeGrand added, with his typical candor, "And I looked around for angels, but I didn't see any."[83]

While LeGrand did not see any angels on this day, a sister present wrote, "The Sunday School passing through the Temple and joining in the 'hosannahs' must have been a sight for angels to gaze upon, and undoubtedly myriads of them were present."[84]

Jane Blood came to Salt Lake with twelve Sunday School children from her ward. "We had such a nice time," she reported. Following the session, Jane walked the children up the short hill near the temple "to see President Young's grave" before returning home on the train.[85]

At each session, the dedicatory prayer was reread by various general Church officers. The meetings were charged with deep feelings, personal reflection, and spiritual power—a sense of the divine pervaded the experience. The time spent in the temple seemed to pass quickly for many, for as one sister wrote about the event, "[the Saints] pass down the granite steps, without the portals, scarcely realizing that hours have passed, for so rapt are they in the events of the moment."[86]

For many of those who attended the dedication services, the occasion was an opportunity to see their beloved leaders, especially their aging prophet, Wilford Woodruff. One brother who had

come a long way to witness the special conference and dedication ceremony stated, "The Brethren all looked good to me, some of them better than I expected, and when I looked at Pres. Woodruff his soul looked white to me."[87] Several decades later, people still recalled what President Woodruff looked like and how he dressed at the dedication, so profound was the effect of seeing him in the temple during this occasion.

During the fourth session of the dedication services, President Woodruff took time to speak on a subject that had caused some Saints to feel unsettled—the issuance of the Manifesto in 1890. "I feel disposed to say something with regard to the Manifesto," he began. "Now I will tell you what was manifested to me and what the Son of God performed in [issuing the Manifesto]," he said to those assembled in the temple.

Yes, I saw by vision and revelation this Temple

*Some twenty-five hundred people gathered at each dedication session and sat on movable chairs
on the main floor and in the balcony of the assembly room.*

79

in the hands of the wicked. I saw our city in the hands of the wicked. I saw every temple in these valleys in the hands of the wicked. I saw great destruction among the people. All these things would have come to pass, as God Almighty lives, had not the Manifesto been given. Therefore, the Son of God felt disposed to have that thing presented to the Church and to the world for purposes in his own mind. The Lord decreed the establishment of Zion. He had decreed the finishing of this temple. He had decreed that the salvation of the living and the dead should be given in these valleys of the mountains.[88]

President Woodruff testified that God had overruled the designs of the evil one; as a result, the Saints could worship freely in the temple and perform the important work of salvation for the dead, one of the prime reasons for building it.

The ceremonies generally met the high expectations of General Authorities and members as they gathered together to worship and to celebrate this important milestone in Church history. A sweet spirit accompanied the meetings at the temple and was a powerful reminder that God was near. President Woodruff noted that "the power of God was manifest in the dedication of this temple and many things [were] revealed by the power of God to the Presidency of the Church."[89]

John Henry Smith recorded in his journal President Woodruff's statement: "The Lord had revealed to him [President Woodruff] that the building was accepted, that if the veil was rent we could see [a] host of heavenly beings."[90]

Wise counsel was given by the Church leadership during and subsequent to the dedication ceremonies. Franklin D. Richards made the following poignant statement on one occasion: "It was more important for the people to be accepted than for the temple to be accepted." President Joseph F. Smith followed up on this theme when he reminded those attending, "Don't be Saints today and sinners tomorrow."[91]

Many in attendance at the dedication services felt a great outpouring of the power of God. Abraham H. Cannon reported, "Many remarkable things were seen and heard in the Temple" during the dedication services. Some saw a great light surrounding the temple, while others "saw brilliant lights, and heard singing and instrumental music" in the temple itself.[92] During one of the sessions, Joseph F. Smith, who had spoken with great power and feelings previously seemed to "have some difficulty in expressing himself with . . . ease and fluency." Suddenly, a light appeared "in front of the Melchizedek Stand" which Joseph F. Smith was speaking from. "At the same instant of this appearance President Smith suddenly spoke with the same potent influence which had characterized his previous addresses." Several in the audience saw this manifestation of the "Spirit of Light."[93]

Lydia Clawson, "while awaiting the commencement of the service [7 April evening session] heard beautiful singing that seemed to come from the South East Corner of the room. At first she thought there must be a choir there, but of course there was not. She heard the singing twice," her husband reported.[94]

Many others, including a nine-year-old boy, saw angels and deceased Church leaders in attendance at the services. Eleven-year-old George Monk, of Payson, Utah, came to the temple with his mother and grandmother. During the service he saw "a man appear at the south-east circular window of the assembly hall of the Temple. This personage looked into the interior." The boy said he then saw several angelic personages enter the temple and described them as the "prettiest men" he had ever seen. They were dressed in "loose flowing white robes [and] most, if not all, had long and somewhat wavy hair." At the close of the meeting, they "suddenly vanished from view."[95]

Hans Jensen Hals's diary emphasized the spiritual nature of the activities associated with the temple dedication: "I and [my] family and two hundred members of the Ward had the privilege to be at the dedication services and had a splendid time. . . . Rich instructions [came] from the authorities [of the Church]. Angels of God were seen coming in the south-east window and sitting on the corners. Two of them moved across the large hall over the people and went out the north window."[96]

Rudger Clawson's wife, Lydia, told him that just before the service began on 10 April she "heard a voice which told her some things about [him]."⁹⁷ Rudger did not reveal in his diary what Lydia told him, if she did at all.

Francis Lyman's journal entry for 17 April included these reflections on the activities of the day: "Elder John W. Taylor spoke nicely [during dedication service]. Thus closed the most glorious day of the Twelve occupied by the dedication services. Our hearts were bursting full. At seven p.m. our Quorum met [for] the second time in our temple room."

During this joyous evening meeting, the brethren shared their feelings, experiences, and testimonies with each other within the walls of the temple. Of the spiritual experiences mentioned, Elder Lyman reported two experiences he had witnessed himself during the day. The first: a "red light [was seen] going across the building above the chandeliers—I saw this," he wrote. He "also heard beautiful music." For this Church leader "it was a very remarkable day."⁹⁸

An unusual incident during the first day of dedication was well reported in numerous personal journals, newspapers, and later recollections of participants—the sudden appearance of sea gulls at the temple. This event caught the attention of many visitors and was reported in the evening edition of the *Deseret Evening News*:

A SINGULAR CIRCUMSTANCE—A Flock of Sea Gulls Hover About the Temple Spires During the Storm. During the violence of the storm today the attention of many people was directed to a flock of about one hundred sea gulls which hovered about the Temple spires. At times the wind would carry them a considerable distance away but as soon as there was a lull they would immediately fly back and circle about the sacred structure which they continued to do until about 12:30, when they disappeared to the northwest.⁹⁹

The ceremonies had a profound impact upon many Saints. For some, the events were a season of rejoicing; for others, they were a time of reconciliation and a new beginning. One young man who had been known for his rowdy behavior reported "a bright halo about the head of [President]

Woodruff." The service was a life-changing experience for the young man, as he reported that the "spirit of the temple was so strong with him that he went home and started a reformation among his companions."¹⁰⁰

Jesse and Emma Smith, who had sought the Lord in prayer, "received assurance" that their sins were forgiven, as Jesse recorded at the time, "realizing my littleness and comparative nothingness." As he entered the temple to participate in the services, he "refrained from food and drink." During one of the sessions, he heard President Woodruff relate a vision he had had "of thousands of Lamanites enter[ing] the temple by the door in the west end of the building previously unknown to him."¹⁰¹

This dedication season had been looked forward to hopefully and longingly by the Saints. The few aged Church leaders and members who were present at the cornerstone dedication some forty years earlier entered the temple with great emotion. Their presence was appreciated by the younger generation. "I greatly enjoyed seeing the greeting of those aged fathers and mothers within the blessed walls, and marked the happiness in their faces as they seemed to say, 'it is finished.'" Annie Wells Cannon noted.¹⁰²

Not only were the living rejoicing at the completion of the temple but also Church authorities believed that many thousands who had already passed to "the other side" were just as joyous, if not more so, with the events of the dedication.

The "Temple Hymn," which was composed and sung on the occasion of the Salt Lake Temple dedication, reveals the deep gratitude the Saints felt as they finally completed their task of finishing the House of the Lord.¹⁰³

Our God, we gladly raise,
Our voices in thy praise.
While here today;
As Saints of latter day.
We offer prayer and praise.
And guide us in thy way.
Oh! God, we pray.

On this, the day of birth
Of one who came to earth
Where millions teem.

And in his name who gave
His precious blood to save,
And triumphed o'er the grave.
Man to redeem.

Accept this house we've reared,
And be thy name revered,
In all the earth;
Soon may thy Zion stand
Upon thy holy land,
Thence by Divine command,
Thy law go forth.

Accept our thanks today,
For flocks and herds we pray.
For fruits and grain;
Soon may thy light increase,
Until all strife will cease.
All men will dwell in peace
And Jesus reign.

An article in the *Woman's Exponent* newspaper in Salt Lake City stated: "How well repaid the saints all feel when they behold the elegance and grandeur of this temple with its massive walls, its frescoed ceilings, its marbled and inlaid floors, its elegantly wrought and carved founts and baths, its soft carpets, its dainty hangings, its art windows, its exquisite furnishings all blending and combining making a *Temple* perfect and complete beyond compare."[104]

One unusual and very notable experience occurred during the services. Emma Bennett of Provo, Utah, gave birth to a son in the temple "just at the close of the evening services" on Friday night, 7 April, near 10:00 P.M.[105] James E. Talmage noted in his diary: "A Sister Bennett from Provo was taken with labor pains and gave easy birth to a son. She was removed from the Assembly Room to a small apartment [in the temple]. Some sects would hold that such an event desecrated the holy place; but the Latter-day Saints will take a directly opposite view."[106]

Eight days later, on 15 April, Emma Bennett returned to the temple with her husband, Benjamin, and new son for a special blessing. In the blessing, Joseph F. Smith named the baby boy Joseph Temple Bennett.

Although many Saints had planned for months to attend the dedication services, one woman who had a young infant did not make any arrangements to attend until just a few hours before the service. She later recalled that during the reading of the dedicatory prayer in one of the sessions, she saw her departed grandfather and a woman whom she did not know. She was inspired to know that she should perform the proxy temple ordinances for the woman. As the vision closed, her grandfather said, "Remember, now remember." The phrase was repeated several times during the remainder of the meetings and was repeated again as she left the temple. Later, while working on her genealogical research, she discovered the name of a previously unknown woman who had been married to her grandfather. The proxy temple work was completed for the woman, and she was sealed to the grandfather.[107]

Several other people had no passes to attend because they were no longer members of the Church, but they requested reconciliation with the Church during the sessions of dedication, still hopeful that they might attend the temple services. For example, a sister from Ogden, Utah, made her request known to L. John Nuttall, President Woodruff's secretary. On 7 April, Brother Nuttall asked President Woodruff "about her and got permission for her to be rebaptized and [for her to] go through the Temple."[108]

Brother Nuttall made arrangements with George Q. Cannon on the particular details for the sister's rebaptism on 9 April. Two days later Brother Nuttall wrote the local priesthood officer about the First Presidency decision and asked him to inform the woman. Eventually she received the joyous news and arrived in Salt Lake City by train on 13 April. She was rebaptized in the Tabernacle baptismal font by Charles Penrose and confirmed a member of the Church by L. John Nuttall himself. Soon thereafter, the sister attended a session of the dedication as a member in full fellowship after years of separation.

The Saints enjoyed their experiences at the Church conference and at the temple dedication services. For many, the occasion was also a time to visit friends and relatives and to gather in reunions. Jesse Smith noted that he "saw hundreds of friends not mentioned" in his journal.[109] Lucy Flake recalled, "I met many old friends I had not seen since I was a girl."[110]

Many had difficulty leaving Salt Lake City—they had enjoyed visiting friends and family members and feeling the spirit of the services, and leaving caused some tears. "There was never such a time of meeting and greeting old friends," Lucy Flake recalled, "but there never was a sweet without a bitter." On 11 April, the Flakes began their return trip. "We bid all our Salt Lake loved ones goodby and started back. . . . It snowed on us all day from Milford to Beaver, and was dreadfully cold." On 13 April, they left Beaver, fearing any further delay would not allow them to cross the "big Colorado" river, which could get "so high we could not cross" it. Finally, after fifteen days, they arrived home and "found all well."[111]

Others, as may be expected, returned to find that life had moved on its natural course. Jesse Smith wrote stoically, "Reached home on the 23rd [April]. My daughter Susie's babe had died during my absence and so had my daughter Sadie's [baby]."[112] Participation in the services seemed to renew the faith of the Saints to confront life's vicissitudes with greater awareness of God's presence in their own lives.

After witnessing a dedication service, Henry Ballard returned to Logan, Utah, in order "to let others go." Sharing responsibilities at home with family members and neighbors allowed Saints to attend sessions that were limited to adults. Henry's brother-in-law, James R. McNeil, and wife soon arrived from New Mexico as they had "come up to attend [the] dedication of the temple and came to Logan and made a visit for a few days."[113]

The Saints returned to their homes feeling rededicated to the Lord and refreshed in the Spirit. The following weeks were spent recounting the experiences of the dedication services to family and friends who were unable to attend. Levi Savage of Santa Clara, Utah, recorded the comments of his bishop who had just arrived from Salt Lake. "Attended Ward meeting in the hall," Savage noted. "Elder George Spilsbury; Levi Harmore and the Bishop just returned from the Salt Lake City Temple Dedication." He continued: "All gave interesting accounts of the magnificent temple; the

proceedings, and the genial spirit manifested every where; even among the Gentiles, also the sea gulls that circled around the spires of the temple during the terrific wind storm that occurred at the time of the dedication."[114]

Many Saints who wanted to attend but were unable were still glad that others, especially friends and family members, did attend the services. Eliza S. Keeler noted: "In April, Sarah, Maggie and Alice had the great privilege of attending the dedication of the temple. Martin was working at [a local hotel] at this time [and] had not the privilege, but desired to go very much so did the rest of us, but I was glad some of [our family] could go anyway."[115]

Wilford Woodruff's dream of dedicating the temple had been fulfilled, but it seemed for a time during the dedication services that his participation during the first week and a half of the services would be his last labors in mortality.

He later recorded, "I attended the dedication of the [temple] on 18 April . . . the last time I attended the dedication [services]." President Woodruff left a priesthood leadership meeting in the temple on 19 April when he "was taken *very sick,* which lasted me on one *month* and fourteen *days* before I went to my desk in the office."[116]

President Woodruff's wife called L. John Nuttall on 21 April to come immediately to the home, "saying they wanted me to go and help President Woodruff as he was very low." Brother Nuttall described the distressing situation in his diary over the next several days, including this entry on 21 April: "I found the president very sick. . . . I spoke to him and he grasped me around the neck like he was in a spasm. I got him quiet. I was alone. His wife came in and was much alarmed. . . . I stayed with the President all night, Brother Asabel Woodruff with me. I bathed the President with alcohol and oil and he slept very nicely."[117]

On the following day Nuttall attended another dedication service and then "went to President Woodruff's and stayed the afternoon and all night. He felt much improved. He asked us to sing in the evening and for us to pray which I did."[118] On 7 May Nuttall reported, "We sang several hymns at President Woodruff's request and he joined in the singing. He was very communicative to me and talked about the temple and [our] former labors

The First Presidency (left to right: George Q. Cannon, First Counselor;
Wilford Woodruff, President; and Joseph F. Smith, Second Counselor)
on the first day of dedication services.

together."[119] Eventually gaining strength, the prophet resumed his duties as President of the Church, and during the following weeks and months he witnessed important events relating to the Church and Utah.

President Woodruff, during the dedication services, prophesied that the Lord would bless the Saints because of their efforts to finish the temple. President Woodruff's efforts in fulfilling his own dreams regarding the Church and Utah were tireless, and his prophecy was fulfilled as his dreams became reality.[120]

Within two months of the temple dedication, the Saltair Beach Resort located at the Great Salt Lake was completed and dedicated. Later that

same summer, Church leaders left Salt Lake City on 29 August to accompany the Tabernacle Choir on a visit to the world's fair, the World Columbian Exposition, held at Chicago, Illinois. The choir received a second-place award in the competition. On 17 October, Wilford Woodruff received a telegram indicating that the government was beginning the process of returning confiscated Church property. In November 1893 the "citizens" gained control of the municipal government in Salt Lake City once again from the minority and anti-Mormon Liberal party.

Another turn of events occurred on 15 November when Judge Charles Zane, Utah Supreme Court Justice, visited Church leaders for the first time. On 13 December the United States Congress passed a bill for the admission of Utah as a state, the first major step towards self-rule in Utah. On 18 December, the Liberal Party disbanded and on the following day ceased to exist.

President Woodruff recorded his reflections of these events in his journal on 31 December 1893:

This is the last of the year of 1893. It has been a very important year in many respects. . . . There have been the greatest changes taken place concerning the Church of Jesus Christ of Latter-day Saints during the year 1893 ever known since its organization. A bill for the admission of Utah into the Union as a state passed the House of Representatives with only five opposing votes. The Mormon Choir took the second prize in the Chicago Fair in contest against the world. Wilford Woodruff, George Q. Cannon and Joseph F. Smith as the Presidency of the Church, was received with open arms at the Chicago Fair by the leading men of the world. Even the mayor and citizens of Jackson County entertained us and made us welcome and all our opponents in Utah have laid down the weapons of war and asked for a state government.[121]

In spite of all the changes and new possibilities before them, for President Woodruff and thousands of others the Salt Lake Temple's completion and dedication was "the greatest event of the year. . . . Great power was manifest on that occasion."[122]

Salt Lake Temple near the time of dedication.

10

"I Have a Mission for You to Fill"

Once the temple was dedicated, a temple presidency and staff needed to be called, set apart, and instructed on their duties as ordinance workers. Many Saints waited patiently for the call to serve. One sister, Lucy B. Young, moved from St. George where she was laboring in the temple to Salt Lake City to be with family. Once in Salt Lake, however, she waited, "looking with longing eyes for the dedication and consequent work in the great temple," an observer noted. "For not until she can enter into her beloved temple work will she ever be happy and satisfied."[1]

Elder Lorenzo Snow was called to act as the first Salt Lake Temple president. He was set apart by the First Presidency on 19 May, just a few weeks following the dedication ceremonies. Susa Young Gates left her description of him while he served in this position: "He stands now at the head of the Temple work in Israel, his beautiful features shining with the light of love and truth, as he walks and works in those sacred halls," she reported. "It is heavenly to see him, surrounded by his fellow-workers, each filled with a measure of his own gentle, sweet forbearance and wisdom, as he sits there presiding over the Saints who assemble to act as saviors upon Mount Zion," she continued. "When you are privileged to go into the Temple, you too will see him [and] you can speak with him, and feel the pressure of his faithful hand."[2]

Zina Diantha Huntington Jacobs Young, Relief Society general president, was called to serve as the president of the female temple workers. A contemporary witness wrote that several weeks before the dedication "[she was] striving to prepare herself, body and mind, for the labor and blessing soon to begin in our latest and most glorious Temple at Salt Lake City."[3]

As the completion of the temple neared, former construction workers were forced to find new employment, as only a few were retained to help prepare the temple for the dedication services. When those services began, the remaining employees were given the time off. Several took temporary positions to help during the services, not knowing if any work would be available following the dedication.

Joseph Henry Dean, who worked in the temple as a carpenter previous to the dedication ceremonies, wrote about his concern for future employment almost daily. He was finally invited back to do some work, but no promises were made for a full-time position. He noted on 2 May 1893, "Worked the fore part of the day in carpenter shop and at noon started down town to get some dinner when I met Apostle Snow who has been appointed president of the Temple."[4] President Snow stopped Joseph and told him that he had wanted to see him. President Snow said, "Brother Dean we have appointed you janitor at the temple . . . if it will be agreeable to you." Joseph was glad to know that a position was available for him and told President Snow, "I should consider any place in the House of the Lord an honorable one, and especially the responsible one he had said they had given me." President Snow then put his hand upon Brother Dean's shoulder and said, "Well Brother Dean, you can go to the House of the Lord and live there and die there if you choose." Brother Dean understood that to mean that he had a job for life if he so desired.[5]

Beginning in early 1893, another brother, Joseph Christenson, "sought the Lord in prayer for a position in the Temple which was soon to be dedicated." About the time of the dedication, George F. Gibbs, a Church secretary, came to him and said he "had been instructed by President Woodruff to say to me that he would like me to apply in writing for a position in the Salt Lake Temple." Brother Christensen recalled: "I filed my application and heard nothing from it until April 25, 1893, when John Nicholson came for me. He told me I was wanted at the Temple. For a month we were busy getting the books ready for the opening [the start of the ordinance work], which took place on the 23rd of May."[6]

Others hoped for an assignment in the temple—not employment, but a call to serve as a volunteer temple ordinance worker. Sarah Jensen, who did not live in Salt Lake City at the time, recalled, "I prayed 'Oh Father permit me once more to work in thy House and all honor be thine.'" A few days later, Sarah was called to an interview with President Snow. "He informed me," Sarah remembered, "that President Woodruff had asked him to preside over the Salt Lake Temple and for him to call the workers and he asked me if I would care to be one of them." Sister Jensen gladly accepted the assignment and moved to Salt Lake City to begin her assignment in the temple. "My heart was full of joy and thankfulness and the splendid time I had there during the summer was great joy. . . . I felt that I loved and was beloved by all our Temple family."[7]

During his illness, Wilford Woodruff began recommending individuals for service in the temple. During a late-night conversation with L. John Nuttall, who was keeping vigil with the prophet through the night, President Woodruff told him that he wanted him to work in the temple. A few days later President Woodruff told Bishop John R. Winder in Brother Nuttall's presence, "I do not know how many brethren I may call to fill a mission on this earth [before I die], but I have a mission for you to fill and that is to be President Assistant to Brother Lorenzo Snow in the Salt Lake Temple." Bishop Winder "did not feel competent to fill the [position]." But President Woodruff protested and said that Bishop

Winder "had labored hard in the completion of the temple and he wished him to fill that position."[8]

President Woodruff wrote a letter to President Snow informing him of the action taken and sent a letter of appointment to Bishop Winder. Others were called and appointed for this special service and were asked to attend a meeting in the temple annex on 16 May 1893.

Mary Ann Freeze, who was living in Salt Lake City, found herself exhausted from the various activities surrounding the temple dedication. At one point she felt near death, but on 6 May 1893, President Snow and his wife, Minnie, visited her home and came directly into the bedroom where she was recovering. "Brother Snow said, 'You haven't got time to be there in bed, we want you at the Temple.'" Sister Freeze was called to attend a meeting at the temple on Saturday.[9]

President Snow wrote to another sister to call her to serve in the temple:

Margaret P. Young, Dear Sister: You have been suggested as one of the workers in the Salt Lake Temple, and are therefore, kindly invited to meet in that building. . . . As it is intended to open the temple for work on Monday May 22nd, you will see the necessity for this invitation being promptly responded to. Come to the east gate, and enter the building by the southwest door. With kind regards, Your brother in the Gospel, Lorenzo Snow. President of the Salt Lake Temple.[10]

At this meeting held in the assembly room of the temple annex, President Lorenzo Snow asked those invited if they were willing to serve as temple workers "as a mission, without remuneration."[11] Sixty-five brethren and sisters were present, and "each being called all responded as being willing and able to do work in the Temple without any pay" and accepted their new assignments.[12] Four days later, John Nicholson, Duncan M. McAllister, Joseph Simmons, and Joseph Christenson were set apart as temple recorders.

The temple leadership consisted of Lorenzo Snow, president; John R. Winder, first assistant; Adolph Madson, second assistant; John Nicholson, chief recorder; Joseph H. Dean, janitor; William

President Lorenzo Snow, the first Salt Lake Temple president, also served as President of the Quorum of the Twelve Apostles at the time.

Crawford, Albert W. Davis, L. John Nuttall, George Romney, Francis Armstrong, L. A. Wilson, Joseph Bull, Wilford Woodruff, Jun., Charles Barrell, James Woodruff, Hugh J. Cannon, Rebecca Slanding, Emma Woodruff, Sarah J. Cannon, Elizabeth G. MacDonald, Sarah J. Jensen, Carolin C.R. Wells, Margaret Taylor, Mary A. Lambert, Lucy B. Young, Harriet A. Preston, Hannah B. Crosby, Mary A. Freeze, Julia L. Smith, Edna L. Smith, Hannah Wells, Dorsette Smith, Mar W. Young, Diana Reid, Mary J. Thompson, Emma Bull, Susan E. Smith, Louisa Miner, Emma O. Salmon, Harriet M. Furoter, Lucy W. Smith, Elizabeth I. Murphy, Alida A. Rockholt, Christina Rockwell, Margaret C. Hull, Margaret A. Caine, Louisa L. Richards, Elizabeth J. Stevenson, Maria W. Wilcox, Clarissa C. Cannon, Elizabeth Webb, Shamira

H. Salmon, doorkeeper; Zina D. H. Young, president of the sisters' department; Bathsheba W. Smith, first assistant; and Minnie J. Snow, second assistant.[13]

During the next few days, weeks and months many individuals were called to labor in the temple:

Jesse W. Fox, Charles J. Thomas, William C. Dunbar, Royal B. Young, Nathaniel Jones, Brigham Y. Hampton, John C. Cutler, Levi W. Richards, John Crawford, Albert W. Davis, Henry F. McCune, Elijah Sheets, Samuel W. Richards, William C. Dunbar, James Sharp, Willard Young, Hyrum Goosbeck, William W. Riler, John Crawford, Morris Young, Andrew Smith, Alexander Burnt, George G. Bywater, John Olsen, William Jeffs, Jen Gravgard, Joseph Kingsbury, Theodore McKean, John

President Zina D. H. Young, first women's department temple president, also served as general president of the Relief Society at the time.

Rossiter, Gersis L. Richards, Lizzie R. Sharp, Amaria Y. Dougull, Phebe Y. Beatie, Zina V. Bull, Maria B. Winder, Minnie J. Snow, Nettie D. Bradford, Harriet A. Taylor, and Alice M. Naisbitt.[14]

On Saturday afternoon, 20 May, members of the First Presidency and Twelve met at the temple at one o'clock. Abraham H. Cannon reported: "I went to the Temple, and assisted in the setting apart of the Temple workers. There being six of the First Presidency and Twelve present, we divided into three parties of two each, I being with President Joseph F. Smith. Thereafter we went through the various rooms, and listened to the ceremonies and dialogues of the same. This occupied our time until five o'clock."[15]

L. John Nuttall, who acted in a dual role as President Woodruff's secretary and a temple recorder, asked to be set apart himself. "I was blessed and set apart," he wrote in his journal, "to labor in the Salt Lake Temple this afternoon by President Lorenzo Snow and John R. Winder." Nuttall continued, "I received [a] very nice blessing. I felt this was necessary although I had been acting as requested."[16]

Now that all the staff had been called, instructed, and set apart, temple service and worship could begin. The first ordinance work, baptism for the dead, commenced in the newly dedicated temple on 22 May, followed by the first temple sealing on 24 May 1893.[17]

On 1 June "over a hundred of [Brigham Young's descendants] did temple work for his dead" progenitors in honor of his birthday anniversary.[18] Soon, many other Latter-day Saints came with their genealogical data to perform proxy ordinances for their deceased family members and also to receive the same ordinances for themselves.

Following the last of the dedication services,

Endowment workers. Bathsheba W. Smith is seated at the left; Zina D. H. Young, center right; and Louisa Green Richards, at the right. These women worked in the Endowment House, and several continued their service in the completed temple. This photograph was taken sometime before the dedication services.

Church leaders met for the first time in their new offices since the dedication on the third floor in the temple on 25 May. Though President Woodruff was unable to attend, the meetings focused on administrative and spiritual concerns. Abraham H. Cannon reported: "At 2 o'clock I met with my Quorum. Present: Father [George Q. Cannon], Joseph F. Smith, Lorenzo Snow, Franklin D. Richards and myself; George F. Gibbs, clerk. We met in the apostles' room in the Temple."[19]

The next few weeks were taken up with administrative meetings in the temple. President Woodruff, still recovering from his sickness, often visited with the brethren briefly to partake of the sacrament, to organize the newly called temple workers, and to answer questions regarding temple ordinances. His journal for Friday, 23 June, notes: "Met with President Snow and the Twelve in the Temple. President Snow talked to the workers. I followed him and talked plainly and gave my views what ought to be done in the temple and how work should be done."[20] Abraham H. Cannon noted, "President Woodruff . . . expressed his pleasure at the work being accomplished in this structure."[21]

President Snow also spoke to the workers in an effort to clarify certain policies and procedures in the meeting. The volunteer temple ordinance workers were "not to impose on the cook by inviting their friends to eat who do not work in the temple. They are not to go out of the door and leave it unlocked in the absence of the doorkeeper, and under no circumstances are they to invite strangers into the building."[22]

Cordial and warm feelings were cultivated between the temple workers and Church leaders as they began to associate regularly within the sacred walls of the temple. On 13 July during a two o'clock First Presidency and Council of the Twelve meeting, Church leaders were surprised when they "were treated to some ice cream by the temple workers."[23] The work of saving the dead and administering an ever-expanding church organization were brought together in the Great Temple.

The women also shared experiences together as they met often in the temple. President Zina Young and the women's temple presidency often called their fellow ordinance workers together "to cultivate a greater feeling of love and sisterly kindness by a better acquaintance with each other."[24] These meetings were well attended and appreciated. One of these sisters left this description of President Zina Young:

It is lovely and an inspiring sight to see this high priestess of righteousness arrayed in her simple white gown of home-made silk, her dark eyes still bright, her delicate face crowned with lustrous bands of shining white hair, her finely-shaped head, with its rich, white lace draping, held erect, as her stately figure moves down the long aisle. The sweet smile of welcome greets all alike in its impartial graciousness. She is indeed the Elect Lady, and wisdom and peace crown her days.[25]

By early summer, the temple became the hub of activity for Church officers. Discussion of business items, doctrinal issues and practices, along with the performance of sacred ordinances, ensured the temple's position as the Saints' focus of religious life in Salt Lake City and beyond.

Finally, the Great Temple was completed and dedicated. "No event in modern times," wrote Emmeline B. Wells, editor of the *Woman's Exponent*,

is so important, and fraught with such momentous consequences to the world and its inhabitants as the opening of this holy edifice for the administration of ordinances that pertain to the living and the dead, to the past and the present, to the endowments and covenants that unite families and kindreds in bonds inseparable. By the Latter-day Saints great things are anticipated in these places of worship, and the revelations of heaven and ministration of angels is a part of the expectation looked forward to and firmly believed in.[26]

Salt Lake Temple during the summer of 1893.

Epilogue

The Salt Lake Temple has come to symbolize in the minds of many the faith and dedication of the members of The Church of Jesus Christ of Latter-day Saints. Although the Saints have built over forty-seven temples during the past one hundred sixty years, the House of the Lord in Salt Lake City is a singularly powerful reminder of the devotion of the early pioneers who came to the Salt Lake Valley many years ago. Temple Square—bounded by Main, South Temple (known earlier as Brigham Street), West Temple, and North Temple streets—historically has been the religious center of the Latter-day Saint faith since the Saints migrated to the Great Basin in 1847. During the first decades following the establishment of Salt Lake City, the Temple Block housed several important places of worship, both public and private.

The temple stands today as a witness of the Lord's promises to a people who sought a place of peace where they could worship according to their own beliefs. The story of its construction and dedication is more than a story of architects, builders, and Church officers; it is one of endless vision, faith, and courage.

The temple's dedication was truly a significant milestone in the history of the Church. The forty years of construction required untold sacrifices. For young sixteen-year-old Joseph Fielding Smith, the time of dedication in 1893 was a notable event. Through his childhood, Joseph watched the daily progress of the temple construction; he later wrote, "In my boyhood anxiety I wondered if I would live to see the temple finished."[1]

Annie Wells Cannon stated at the time of the temple's dedication in 1893:

I am only one of thousands who have watched the rearing of those walls and seemed to be a part of them, so much have our thoughts dwelt upon and longed for the day of completion. . . . This dedication is to the Saints the greatest event for many years. How long we have watched the building of the Temple and as stone has been laid upon stone our faith and prayers have been offered for the safe and perfect completion of the building and now that it is so handsomely completed well may we feel proud and happy.[2]

The temple, completed and dedicated on the fortieth anniversary of the laying of the cornerstones, is a symbol of purity, peace, and oneness with God.

One of the first acts of the Saints upon entering the Salt Lake Valley in 1847 was to identify the temple site. President Brigham Young pushed for the completion of this remarkable building constantly throughout his life. Though the temple was not completed before his death in 1877, the vision of the Great Salt Lake Temple with its six main spires, echoing the granite peaks to the east from where Brigham had first looked down on the promised land, remained constantly before him as the temple was being built, just a few hundred yards west of his home. Brigham Young had brought the Lord's people across the wilderness to a promised land. Now their duty was to build a sacred house to the Lord's name.

President Young reminded the Saints in 1863 of their duty to complete the temple when he said, "There is not a house on the face of the whole

*Salt Lake Temple Block, with landscaping completed and monument in honor of
Brigham Young and the early pioneers temporarily located in center of lawn.
This monument was later moved to its present location at the intersection of Main
and South Temple streets. At lower right is the Orson Pratt Observatory.*

earth that has been reared to God's name and which will in anywise compare with his character, and that he can consistently call his house." President Young went on to prophesy what would have seemed utterly ludicrous to any visitor to the struggling Mormon colony—that not only would the Salt Lake Temple be completed but also "there will be hundreds of [temples] built and dedicated to the Lord."[3]

Brigham Young's prophecy is now being fulfilled. The Saints' sacred duty to redeem the dead through the proxy temple ordinances has caused them to continue to erect other sacred temples, not only in North America but also around the world. Among these edifices, the Salt Lake Temple will always remain a symbol of the vision and industry of the people of God who were led to their promised land by an American Moses, Brigham Young.

The Saints built the Salt Lake Temple as part of their preparations for the millennial day, when Jesus Christ will return to the earth and establish peace for a thousand years. The vision of Micah, one Old Testament prophet who saw the promised millen-nial day, included the establishment of the House of the Lord in the "tops of the mountains." The Latter-day Saints believe that the construction and dedication of the Salt Lake Temple in the Rocky Mountains is a partial fulfillment of that vision:

But in the last days it shall come to pass, that the mountain of the house of the Lord shall be established in the top of the mountains, and it shall be exalted above the hills; and people shall flow unto it.

And many nations shall come, and say, Come, and let us go up to the mountain of the Lord, and to the house of the God of Jacob; and he will teach us of his ways, and we will walk in his paths: for the law shall go forth of Zion, and the word of the Lord from Jerusalem.

And he shall judge among many people, and rebuke strong nations afar off; and they shall beat their swords into plowshares, and their spears into pruninghooks: nation shall not lift up a sword against nation, neither shall they learn war any more.

But they shall sit every man under his vine and under his fig tree; and none shall make them afraid: for the mouth of the Lord of hosts hath spoken it. (Micah 4:1-4; see also Isaiah 2:2-5.)

An editorial in the *Juvenile Instructor* emphasized this belief: "The most momentous event in the history of the Latter-day Saints has just been consummated. The great Temple at Salt Lake City, concerning which both ancient and modern prophets have spoken and written, is completed and dedicated to the Most High."[4]

On a personal level, the completion and dedication of the temple meant introspection and a renewed awe at the Lord's majesty and love. B. H. Roberts noted: "This has been a pentecostal time with me. The Lord has shown me my inner parts, myself; and there I have found such grained and gnarled spots that I have been humbled to sincere repentance. At times I have wondered even how the Lord could tolerate me at all as His servant. Truly it is a manifestation of long suffering and mercy."[5]

Even today, for those who walk the grounds of the Salt Lake Temple or participate in temple worship, a feeling of humility and thanksgiving to a merciful God is evoked as people look at the temple spires rising toward heaven—symbolic of men's and women's reaching toward a loving Father in Heaven, who willingly extends his arms in return. For others, the temple represents another symbol. Samuel Adams, a participant in the 1853 cornerstone laying, the 1892 capstone laying, and the April 1893 dedication ceremonies, wrote that the temple is a "stepping stone to Heaven."[6]

The events of one hundred years ago were much more than the dedication of a building. They represent the dedication of an entire people to God. As long as the Saints continue to exhibit such devotion, the temple, rising towards heaven like the mountains around it, rests on a foundation more secure than the cornerstones so carefully placed "beneath the reach of mountain floods"—it rests on the foundation of faith, the living rock the early pioneers planted more than one hundred and forty years ago.

Salt Lake Temple, east facade.

Appendix:
The Design of the Salt Lake Temple

The construction of the Salt Lake Temple was one of the most ambitious and important undertakings by the Saints during the nineteenth century.[1] The *New York Times* noted in its 7 April 1893 edition:

> The Mormon Temple is a significant monument in enduring stone to the power and resistless growth of the Mormon Church. Imposing in size, its architecture is impressive only because it conveys the sense of ponderous masses piled high, with all the strong effect of masonry showing lofty vertical lines. The architecture suggests Gothic instincts in general effect, but if one looks for any single detail of the schools he cannot find one. The building is barbaric in its simplicity and freedom from the traditions of any school of architecture; it is imposing and frowning because of the rude strength of its masses superimposed.

"Brigham Young conceived the design," the paper declared, "presumably through inspiration of some unnatural power, for no such building is to be seen elsewhere in any quarter of the globe."[2] The *Salt Lake Herald* announced that the completed temple was "One of the World's Wonders." This was not a mere boast of a proud people, but as the article continued, "Not the Latter-day Saints alone, but all residents of the region view the Salt Lake Temple with pride." The temple was "stately" and "magnificent," according to the news reporter.[3] Church architect Truman O. Angell, Sr., and his assistant, William Ward, took Brigham Young's vision of the temple and made it a concrete reality.[4]

"To the Editor of the Deseret News," Truman O. Angell wrote in 1854. What followed was the first written description of the temple (later, the plan was revised and republished in 1874). This account was reproduced in various newspapers and made its way to England, where members of the Church began to learn for the first time the magnitude of the undertaking. Realizing that the published description would not satisfy everyone, Angell pleaded, "For further particulars wait till the house is done, then come and see it."[5]

The structure is a mixture of classical styles, including Gothic, but is unique and distinctive in its combination of design. Although the outside design of the temple, such as the six towers, remained almost unchanged from the original drawings, the interior layout and the details of many exterior symbolic motifs were either removed or altered over the forty-year construction period.

The most common building material in Utah during the mid-1850s was adobe. Good quality adobe clay was easily found, the insulating qualities were exceptional, and an individual could make several thousand adobe bricks within a short period of time. For these reasons and others, President Young thought the temple should be built with adobe walls.

Within a short time, however, the planned use of adobe was changed to granite found near Salt Lake City in Little Cottonwood Canyon. Along with the change in building material came the first rendering of what the temple would look like when completed.

At the dedication of the temple in 1893, the following dimensions were published:

Length of the building.....................186.5 feet
Width of the building ....99 feet
Height of central east tower
 (including spire) ....222.5 feet
Height of central west tower
 (including spire) ....219 feet
Height of side east towers
 (including spire) ....200 feet
Height of side west towers
 (including spire.........................194 feet
Height of walls ....167.5 feet
Thickness of walls at bottom ....9 feet
Thickness of walls at top ....6 feet
Thickness of buttresses.........................7 feet

The footing wall was sixteen feet thick and eight feet deep. The building in 1893 covered an area of 21,850 feet. Following the capstone-laying celebration, the *Deseret Weekly* published a full description of the temple. It concluded:

In viewing this magnificent structure as it stands today, a triumph of architecture, the fact should not be lost sight of that the designs were made and the work commenced under the most unfavorable circumstances. Only when we remember this can we form an idea of the heroic faith that prompted the first builders and the unselfish sacrifices that made its erection possible.

The article compared the wealth and numerical strength of the people of ancient Israel during the construction of its magnificent temples of Solomon, Zerubbabel, and Herod to that of the pioneer Saints:

But what had the Saints when they dedicated the ground on which this magnificent structure stands? Let the history of the pioneers answer that question. These noble Saints found themselves in a desert, hundreds of miles from a civilization, from which they had been compelled to flee for their lives. They were destitute with all that this word implies, and they were few in number. Yet, they trusted in Him who had led them to this valley and in His name the work was carried on. It should be ev-

ident to all that the blessings of the Almighty have been showered upon this country as a token of his acceptance of the faith and sacrifices of His people. The contemplation of this fact fills the hearts of the faithful ones with joy and they cannot but render to Him the honor and the glory for what has been accomplished, anticipating at the same time many blessings yet in store for the Saints of the Most High.[6]

The building described by architect Angell in 1854 and the description published in the *Deseret Weekly* in 1892 were somewhat different, both in the interior and exterior features.

The most unique exterior feature of the great temple was the six spires. The first three LDS Temples (Kirtland, Nauvoo, and St. George) had only one; the next two temples (Logan and Manti) featured two towers. The original plans for the Salt Lake Temple called for weather vanes on top of the six wooden spires, but the finished temple had stone spires and a gold-leafed statue of the angel Moroni atop the highest spire, the central east tower. The *Chicago Tribune* reported in 1893 that the statue was of "admirable proportions and graceful poise. . . . It is clearly outlined against the mountain tops and can be seen many miles away."[7]

The other towers were capped with a copper finial. Each finial was ringed by eight incandescent bulbs that illuminated the towers of the building. In its description of the temple, the *San Francisco Chronicle* stated: "Its polished towers and glittering spires can be seen far down the valley. All are lighted with electricity. Even Moroni, whose statue, fourteen feet high covered with gold-leaf, surmounts the capstone of the highest central tower, bears upon his crown an electric jet of 300-candle power."[8]

The capstone on which Moroni stands and the granite block upon which it rests form a sphere. Under this capstone was laid a finely polished copper plate engraved by David McKenzie with the following information upon it:

HOLINESS TO THE LORD
The Temple Block Consecrated and
Ground Broken for the
Foundation of This Temple, February 14th, 1853

The Corner Stones
Were Laid April 6th, 1853,
Commencing at the Southeast Corner

GENERAL CHURCH AUTHORITIES
April 6, 1853

First Presidency—Brigham Young, Heber C. Kimball, Willard Richards

Twelve Apostles—Orson Hyde, Parley P. Pratt, Orson Pratt, Wilford Woodruff, John Taylor, George A. Smith, Amasa M. Lyman, Ezra T. Benson, Charles C. Rich, Lorenzo Snow, Erastus Snow, Franklin D. Richards

Patriarch to the Church—John Smith, son of Asael

First Seven Presidents of Seventies—Joseph Young, Levi W. Hancock, Henry Herriman, Zera Pulsipher, A. J. Rockwood, Jedediah M. Grant, Benjamin L. Clapp

Presiding Bishop—Edward Hunter

T. O. Angell, Jos. D. C. Young, architects

April 6th 1892

First Presidency—Wilford Woodruff, George Q. Cannon, Joseph F. Smith

Twelve Apostles—Lorenzo Snow, Franklin D. Richards, Brigham Young, Francis M. Lyman, George Teasdale, John W. Taylor, Anthon H. Lund, Moses Thatcher, John H. Smith, Heber J. Grant, Marriner W. Merrill, Abraham H. Cannon

Patriarch to the Church—John Smith, son of Hyrum

First Seven Presidents of Seventies—Jacob Gates, Seymour B. Young, C. D. Fjeldsted, John Morgan, B. H. Roberts, George Reynolds, Jonathan G. Kimball

Presiding Bishop—William B. Preston

Robert T. Burton, John R. Winder, counselors

The capstone was laid April 6th 1892, by President Wilford Woodruff

The temple's east facade includes several stones of symbolic design and significance. Ascending from the ground level are the earth stones, moon stones, sun stones, star stones, and Saturn stones. The earth, moon, and sun stone motifs represent the three degrees of glory—the telestial, terrestrial, and celestial kingdoms of heaven (see 1 Corinthians 15:40-42). At one time, it was planned to gild the points of the sun stone and to shade the disc area so as to give the stone a golden gleam. Whether this was ever done is not known.

Another feature of the east facade is the angel Moroni statue with Moroni blowing his trumpet to herald the proclamation of the everlasting gospel to the nations of the earth (see Revelation 14:6).

Other motifs include the cloud stones, which may represent the presence of God as used in the Old and New Testaments (see 1 Kings 8:10; Matthew 17:5), and the dedicatory inscription, consisting of a surface a little over twenty feet by six feet of letters deeply cut and heavily gilded. The inscription reads:

HOLINESS TO THE LORD
The House of the Lord, built by
the Church of Jesus Christ
of Latter-day Saints
Commenced April 6, 1853
Completed April 6, 1893

Just below the dedicatory inscription is found the all-seeing eye, a symbol of God's omnipresent nature and divine protection (see Psalm 33:18; Proverbs 15:3). There is some evidence that this stone, along with the handclasp motif stone, were originally painted.[9] The alpha-omega inscription on the keystone (Revelation 1:8) is an affirmation of Jesus Christ's eternal existence; and the handclasp motif, representing the giving of the "right hand of fellowship," falls below the all-seeing eye.

The west facade of the temple, in place of the dedicatory inscription found on the east facade, contains the seven stars of the northern constellation Ursa Major, otherwise known as the Big Dipper, with the pointers ranging nearly toward the North Star. The symbolic meaning of this motif is, "the lost may find themselves by way of the priesthood."[10] Around the entire temple, the fifty moon stones display the cycle of a lunar month—new, first-quarter, full, and last-quarter moons for the 1878 year.

The four great doorways, two at each end, are eight feet wide and just over sixteen feet high. The

Above: All-seeing eye motif on east facade of central tower.

At right: Doorknob from Salt Lake Temple with beehive, "Holiness to the Lord," and hand-clasp motifs.

Below: Alpha-omega and handclasp motifs on east facade of central tower.

doors themselves are twelve feet high, and each single door is four feet wide. The hardware attachments are of special design and made of cast bronze. The doorknob shows in relief the beehive, and above it in a curved line are the words *Holiness to the Lord* (Zechariah 14:20-21). The escutcheon presents in relief the clasped hands within a wreath of olive twigs, an arch with keystone, and the dates "1853-1893."

An original feature related to the east-entrance staircase and doors is two sculpture niches. The niches on either side of the east central towers originally contained the bronze statues of Joseph and Hyrum Smith. The statues stood in these niches until 1911, when they were removed and placed on granite plinths on the lawn south of the temple. The bronze statues of the martyred Church leaders were sculpted by Mahonri M. Young. The statues were originally placed below the "alpha and omega" keystone and above the earth stones—perhaps signifying that the prophets, under Christ, were given authority to administer to the inhabitants of the earth.

The iconographic meanings of the symbolic representations on the exterior of the temple are often only hinted at in early Church publications and statements by Church officers. In several cases, the precise meaning attached to each is impossible to discern. Nonetheless, these representations were meant to reinforce the spiritual teachings revealed in the ordinances performed in the temple. President George A. Smith wrote, "Every one conveys a moral lesson, and all point to the celestial world."[11]

The earliest architectural drawings of the temple exterior show detailed aspects of the many symbols. The change from the freestone veneer, originally intended for the exterior, to granite eliminated the ability to include these fine details; nevertheless, the main features remained the same.

The temple interior design witnessed the most significant changes during the planning and construction. Originally, the plans called for a design similar to that of the first three temples in Ohio, Illinois, and St. George, Utah—two major floors with large assembly halls, the required double set of pulpits in each hall, and an "attic" story for offices and meeting rooms. Eventually, this design was dropped in favor of the current arrangement

of rooms. Nevertheless, a general assembly floor with priesthood tiered pulpits remained an important part of the space allocation. However, the pulpits were placed in the attic section, now part of a full three-story elevation.

Before his death, President Young told the Church architect, William H. Folsom, "that he intended to have the Manti and Logan temple alike, that is the inside, for plans of convenience of performing the labors [temple ordinances and ceremonies] therein."[12] The change of interior room configuration in the Logan and Manti temples resulted in the change of the interior arrangement of the Salt Lake Temple, then under construction.

One participant at the dedication services in 1893 wrote, "It would be in vain for me to attempt a description of the interior of the Temple or to describe the heavenly feeling that pervaded all the [rooms]."[13] Henry Ballard wrote that the interior was the most beautiful building "I had ever beheld upon earth, seemingly to be in heaven."[14] The highly detailed and luxuriously decorated interior stands in stark contrast to the monumental nature of the exterior.

The temple interior, when completed in 1893, was made up of several floors, including a basement area where the baptistry is located. The baptismal font room occupies the west half of the basement. The baptismal font holds nearly five hundred gallons of water to facilitate baptism by complete immersion. The font itself rests on the

Temple baptismal font.

backs of twelve cast-iron oxen, representing the twelve tribes of Israel (1 Kings 7:23-26).

Separate rooms are provided for the presentation of the endowment, "each devoted to a particular part of the course."[15] The garden room is located in the basement area. Its visual impact was noted in the 7 April 1893 edition of the *Salt Lake Herald:*

It is upon the first floor that the magnificence and splendor of the decorations and furnishings burst upon the spectator, who passes in wonder and amazement from one scene of beauty to visions still more enchanting. The "Garden of Eden" or "Creation" room, is located to the west of the grand staircase. In this room [garden room] the genius of the artist has transferred vividly realistic scenes to the walls and ceilings. Forest scenery, streams, mountains and wild beasts are depicted with such marvelous skill and startling effect that the spectator is almost convinced that he is standing in the midst of the creation wilds. This room is furnished with stationary seats and richly carpeted.

From the garden room a stairwell leads to the telestial, or world, room. The telestial room occupies the southwest quadrant of the second floor of the building over the baptistry. The next room, the terrestrial room, is located on the second floor of the temple. "The Terrestrial room is more beautiful than any yet described," the *Salt Lake Herald* continued its description. "Decorated entirely in white and gold, it presents a scene of chaste loveliness that fills the soul with delight. . . . A mammoth French plate mirror is placed on the west side, and several oil paintings by master hands adorn the walls." Here one may also see the veil of the temple.

The veil is located in the terrestrial room and is symbolic of the veil mentioned in the Bible (Exodus 26:33). The veil separates the terrestrial room from the celestial room. The celestial room, the larger of these rooms, represents the kingdom of God. It is beautifully decorated, and its spaciousness is in marked contrast to the preceding rooms. The *Salt Lake Herald* account continued:

Celestial room of the temple.

The Celestial room is the crowning glory of the Temple, it absolutely defies description. The travelers who have visited many lands and gazed upon all the palatial splendors of the earth, declare that they have seen nothing that equals the magnificence of this room. It is truly all that its name indicates—celestial. . . . The ceiling, which is of lofty height and arched, is of marvelous beauty, and an inspired genius surely worked out its creation. Ten stately Grecian columns, richly carved, are ranged on the north and south sides. . . . Three magnificent French plate mirrors adorn the east wall. A narrow flight of stairs in the northeast corner lead to the President's room.[16]

Located on this same floor are also several sealing ordinance rooms. Here a couple kneel at an altar and are married or sealed for time and eternity by temple sealers having special priesthood authority to perform such ordinances.

An even more sacred room is located just off the celestial room between two sealing rooms and is reached by a short ascent from the main floor. This room, the Holy of Holies, corresponds to the Holy of Holies of the Old and New Testament temples (1 Kings 6:16).

The next floor, the third floor, is reserved for administrative councils of the Church. The six separate rooms, known as the council chambers, on this floor are furnished for the presidencies of the various quorums of the priesthood. Here the leadership of the Church meets regularly to conduct the business of the Church, to hold testimony meetings, and to partake the sacrament of the Lord's Supper.

The most striking of these council chambers are the rooms of the First Presidency and of the Twelve Apostles. The General Authorities themselves paid for the furniture in these rooms. On 11 April 1893, the First Presidency and Council of the Twelve met in these rooms following the first dedication service. Elder Marriner Merrill noted, "The Twelve had a short meeting at 1 p.m. and subscribed $1,800.00 to pay for the furniture in our room in the Temple. I paid $150.00 today."[17]

In one of the former apartments is another Tiffany and Company stained-glass window called the Memorial Window. It depicts the completed Salt Lake Temple, over which appears the motto, "Holiness to the Lord." An inscription on the left reads: "Corner stone laid April 6, 1853, by President Brigham Young, assisted by his counselors, Heber C. Kimball, Willard Richards." Another on the right makes this record: "Dedicated April 6, 1893, by President Wilford Woodruff, assisted by his counselors, George Q. Cannon, Joseph F. Smith."

Located on the top floor, the fourth floor, between the two tower complexes is the main assembly room or hall. This room is by far the largest in the temple, measuring one hundred twenty feet by eighty feet. At both ends of the assembly hall floor are four-tiered stands. Similar stands were incorporated into the design of the first two Latter-day Saint temples in Ohio and Illinois and the three Utah temples at St. George, Logan, and Manti.

The temple complex at Salt Lake City had two other buildings constructed nearby that were important to its operation, the temple annex and heating plant. The temple annex was built some one hundred feet north of the temple proper at the time of the completion of the temple itself. The annex and the temple were connected by a semi-subterranean passage. The annex design was somewhat different from what had been incorporated into previous Mormon architectural projects, including the Salt Lake Temple. The annex was de-

signed by Joseph Don Carlos Young in the popular Victorian version of the Byzantine style of Eastern Orthodox Church tradition.

For the temple annex, architect Young used sandstone from Sanpete County, from the same quarry from which the stone for the Manti Temple was taken. The annex was used as the main entrance to the temple and was connected with the temple by a magnificent corridor twelve feet wide, which was brilliantly illuminated by two hundred incandescent lights. The cost of this structure was estimated at about sixty thousand dollars.

An article printed about the time of the dedication services noted:

The term "Annex" will thus be seen to have another meaning than that of an insignificant and inferior appendage. In this case the natural thought is that the Annex is almost a Temple of itself, so chaste, pure, artistic and elegant are its general design and internal appointments. It is not extravagant to say that nothing in the country of its size and cost surpasses it in unique and pleasing style and excellence of workmanship. It is a real gem, and reflects abundant credit upon, as it will ever constitute a monument to the taste and skill of Architect Young.[18]

The temple heating plant, or boiler house, was constructed three hundred feet north of the northwest corner of the temple. It was built of stone from Spanish Fork Canyon. In its basement were four large boilers, two for generating steam and two for generating hot water. The process for heating the temple was known as Mills automatic system, which utilized hot water. The two steam boilers operated four Edison dynamos to generate electricity to light the temple.

The temple was fitted with the most up-to-date heating and electrical conveniences, many of which were unthinkable when the temple was first designed. For some, the fact that the temple took so long in completion was a manifestation of the hand of God:

While this Temple was under way, sanitary science stepped from infancy almost to maturity, this, together with the latest improvements in heating will add immensely to the comfort, convenience and cleanliness of the many thousands who will work there for the living and the dead. The electric lights, that "modern miracle," will aid in giving beauty to both the interior and exterior, such as was undreamed of until the later years of construction. Many other items suggest themselves which are among modern improvements in a mechanical and decorative direction. . . . Every hindrance ultimately tends to show that there is an overruling hand, and that in the order of God, through his servants, the house, finally completed will be more worthy of its Divine character, will more fully represent the progress and prosperity of Israel, and will testify more loudly to the world of those principles which from the corner-stone, to the flashing light above Moroni's head, suggest "Peace on earth and good will to man."[19]

During the open house and dedication services, people were able to take a tour of the temple's interior. Individuals had been placed at key locations to explain the individual rooms and some of the features that distinguished the area from others in the temple. Among those features shown to the visitors was an elevator, a modern invention not originally planned for the building. This proved useful to those attending the dedication sessions who were physically unable to take the long walking tour through the building.

L. John Nuttall took a family member "to the temple and up the elevator. [I] got her a good seat in the Aaronic stand [in the Assembly Room] so she could enjoy the services. She would not walk through the house" because of a disability.[20] The modern conveniences added to the quality of usefulness of the building; nevertheless, George Q. Cannon noted just days before the dedication ceremonies in 1893:

The completion of a Temple means more to our minds than the mere finishing of a costly pile of masonry. It means that an enduring bond of unity between time and eternity has been welded; it means that the heavens are brought that much nearer the earth; it means that the faith which enables a people to honor God in keeping these his commandments will enable them also to prevail mightily with him in securing their own salvation and the redemption of mankind.[21]

Three Church Presidents (Brigham Young, John Taylor, and Wilford Woodruff), several Church architects and assistants (Truman O. Angell, Sr., William Ward, William H. Folsom, Truman O. Angell, Jr., and Joseph Don Carlos Young), and countless craftsmen and workers contributed to the design, construction, and final architectural beauty of the Salt Lake Temple.

Since its dedication in 1893, the Salt Lake Temple has witnessed numerous cosmetic changes to incorporate modern electrical, heating, and cooling systems; to replace the original annex; and to attach an annex with additional sealing rooms to the north wall of the temple. Elder ElRay L. Christiansen, an assistant to the Council of the Twelve and Salt Lake Temple president from 1954 to 1962, recommended major renovations of the temple to make these changes beginning in 1958. The generation who had participated in the construction and dedication of the temple expressed some concern about what changes were being made and how they would affect the building.

In 1965, an elderly brother recalled that as a ten-year-old boy he had found employment on a nearby farm where, after several long hours of work, he was paid twenty-five cents. "I clutched the coin and ran home," he recalled. He immediately sought out his father. "Pa, look what I have!" he announced. "The next time you go to Provo," he continued, "I can get a new pair of Levis with this money."[22]

The father reminded his son of President Woodruff's request for funds to complete the temple on time. "President Wilford Woodruff needs ten cents of this quarter for the Salt Lake Temple. Here, I'll give you fifteen cents for the coin, and we'll go together to give the dime to our bishop, who will send it to Salt Lake City," the father gently suggested. The funds were collected, the work was completed, and the temple was dedicated in 1893.

The aged gentleman paused for a moment or two after relating his own personal story of sacrifice and then asked those who were renovating the temple, "Now what have [you] been doing to the Salt Lake Temple?" Assured that the same care was being shown during the remodeling of the temple as had been demonstrated by the nineteenth-century Saints, the elderly man felt that the building which prompted his sacrifice seventy years earlier as a young boy was not being disturbed or unduly modified.

One of the significant changes was the erection of a new temple annex. The new annex, located on the north side of the temple itself, was erected with original temple granite from Little Cottonwood Canyon. The annex chapel has two murals painted by Harris T. Weberg. The first portrays the city of Jerusalem during the time of the mortal ministry of Christ. The second, the "Ascension of the Resurrected Christ," is located on the north wall of the chapel, directly behind the rostrum.

When the temple was first dedicated in 1893, Andrew Jenson wrote at the conclusion of the first dedication service, "Thus was dedicated the largest and most magnificent Temple erected by the Latter-day Saints in the 19th century. Glory to God in the highest!"[23]

For the Latter-day Saints all temples, regardless of their size or location, are special and holy. Nevertheless, the Salt Lake Temple remains symbolic of the nineteenth-century Saints' courage and sacrifice. Architecturally and structurally, the fourth-floor assembly room was a feature common to all nineteenth-century temples built by the Saints. The presence of the Holy of Holies and administrative offices and rooms in the Salt Lake Temple, however, make this temple unique.

The *San Francisco Chronicle* stated in its 7 April 1893 issue:

The temple is the greatest landmark in Mormondom. It is to Salt Lake and the Mormons what St. Peter's is to Rome and the Catholics. It is a massive structure, and stands as a monument of the united efforts of a peculiar and powerful sect of religionists. . . . The whole represents the free will offering of a frugal and industrious and, at one time, poverty stricken people. The completion of this temple is the crowning event in their history. Many of their old and wise men have lived for that alone and now declare that they can die content. Even Wilford Woodruff, their gray-haired president, who is vigorous and bright at 87, says he is now ready to die.[24]

The non-Mormon press praised the Saints' efforts in constructing a beautiful building and rightfully identified it as a "monument of united effort," but the temple is more than that.

B. H. Roberts reflected on the meaning of the temple for him during a Church conference shortly before his death:

Whenever I pass this Temple, walk alongside of it and contemplate its towers, its architectural beauty . . . I hold it as sacred in my heart as I look upon it; and I have another thought in connection with it, and that is that it is a mass testimony of a whole people, a testimony to the world that God has spoken, and that he has revealed his truths once more for the salvation of men and has ushered in the dispensation of the fulness of times. It is . . . a community testimony of the gospel of Jesus Christ, and becomes a witness wherever even the counterfeit presentment of its architectural beauty is published to the world. I love the temple as a testimony to the world of God's great new dispensation of his gospel, and the other temples also partake of the same glory and power and spirit.[25]

The Salt Lake Temple is truly, as B. H. Roberts eloquently stated, "a testimony to the world that God has spoken."

Notes

The abbreviations listed below have been used to simplify references in the notes that follow:

HBLLBYU — Harold B. Lee Library, Brigham Young University, Provo, Utah

HLSMC — Huntington Library, San Marino, California; all material from HLSMC is reproduced with permission

House of the Lord (1893) — *House of the Lord: Historical and Descriptive Sketch of the Salt Lake Temple* (Salt Lake City: Geo. Q. Cannon and Sons Co., Publishers, 1893)

JD — *Journal of Discourses*, 26 vols. (London: Latter-day Saints' Book Depot, 1854-1886)

JH — Journal History of The Church of Jesus Christ of Latter-day Saints, LDS Church Archives

LDS Church Archives — Archives Division, Church Historical Department, The Church of Jesus Christ of Latter-day Saints, Salt Lake City, Utah; all material from LDS Church Archives is used with permission

Millennial Star — *The Latter-day Saints' Millennial Star*

MLUU — J. Willard Marriott Library, University of Utah, Salt Lake City, Utah

Truman O. Angell, Journal 1851-1856 — Truman O. Angell, "A Journal of My Time Kept by My Own Hand," commencing 15 December 1851, typescript, LDS Church Archives

Truman O. Angell, Journal 1857-1868 — Truman O. Angell, Journal 1857, 8 April 1867-1868, LDS Church Archives

USHS — Library Archives, Utah State Historical Society, Salt Lake City, Utah

---

Preface

1. A list of workers accidently killed during the temple construction has previously been published (see W. A. Raynor, *The Everlasting Spires: A Story of the Salt Lake Temple* [Salt Lake City: Deseret Book Co., 1965], pp. 117-18). Upon further investigation, however, several death dates have been found to be incorrect, and one worker mentioned, William McCiban, was working on the New Tabernacle rather than the temple as indicated (see *Deseret News,* 28 May 1878). Sam Kaealoi and Samuel Ensign were not included on the list, but their obituaries indicate that they died while working on the temple (see *Deseret News,* 27 September 1878 and *Deseret Evening News,* 25 June 1885).

2. Sermon of Brigham Young, delivered in the Bowery in Salt Lake City, Utah, 6 October 1863, *JD* 10:254.

3. "A Great Temple," *Juvenile Instructor* 28 (15 April 1893): 241.

Chapter 1. "God Gathers Together His People in the Last Days"

1. Joseph Smith, *Teachings of the Prophet Joseph Smith,* sel. Joseph Fielding Smith (Salt Lake City: Deseret Book Co., 1938), 308.

2. For a discussion of Mormon settlement in Missouri and the plat of the city of Zion, see Richard Neitzel Holzapfel and T. Jeffery Cottle, *Old Mormon Kirtland and Missouri: Historic Photographs and Guide* (Santa Ana: Fieldbrook Productions, Inc., 1991), 157-208.

3. For a discussion of the Latter-day Saints' efforts to build and dedicate the Kirtland Temple, and for a photographic essay on the temple, see Holzapfel and Cottle, *Old Mormon Kirtland,* 27-76, 135-53.

4. For a discussion of the Nauvoo Temple and the establishment of the Church center in Illinois, see Richard Neitzel Holzapfel and T. Jeffery Cottle, *Old Mormon Nauvoo and Southeastern Iowa: Historic Pho-*

tographs and Guide (Santa Ana: Fieldbrook Productions, Inc., 1991), 11-24, 34-39.

5. Two books—John K. Edmunds, *Through Temple Doors* (Salt Lake City: Bookcraft, 1978) and Boyd K. Packer, *The Holy Temple* (Salt Lake City: Bookcraft, 1980)—offer personal testimony of the blessings of temple worship in the Church today and explain in general terms the special ordinances and sacred ritual conducted therein.

6. While it was Joseph Smith's desire to complete the temple in Nauvoo, Brigham Young, as President of the Twelve, "inquired of the Lord whether we should stay here and finish the Temple. The answer was we should." (See Holzapfel and Cottle, *Old Mormon Nauvoo and Southeastern Iowa,* 126.)

7. B. H. Roberts, ed., *History of The Church of Jesus Christ of Latter-day Saints,* 7 vols. (Salt Lake City: The Church of Jesus Christ of Latter-day Saints, 1932-51), 7:562.

8. *Deseret Evening News,* 26 July 1880.

Chapter 2. "Here We Shall Build a Temple to Our God"

1. "Interesting items concerning the Journeying of the Latter-day Saints from the city of Nauvoo, until their location in the valley of the Great Salt Lake (Extracted from Private Journal of Orson Pratt)," *Millennial Star* 12 (5 June 1850): 178.

2. Wilford Woodruff, Journals 1833-1898, 24 July 1946, LDS Church Archives. A published typescript is Wilford Woodruff, *Wilford Woodruff's Journals: 1833-1898 Typescript,* ed. Scott G. Kenney. 9 vols. (Midvale: Signature Books, 1985).

3. Ibid., 27 July 1846.

4. Elden J. Watson, ed., *Manuscript History of Brigham Young 1846-1847* (Salt Lake City: Elden J. Watson, 1971), 567.

5. JH, 28 July 1847.

6. Sermon of Brigham Young, delivered in the Old Tabernacle in Salt Lake City, Utah, 6 April 1853, *JD* 1:133.

7. For information on William Weeks, see J. Earl Arrington, "William Weeks, Architect of the Nauvoo Temple," *Brigham Young University Studies* 19 (Spring 1979): 337-59.

8. B. H. Roberts, ed., *History of The Church of Jesus Christ of Latter-day Saints,* 7 vols. (Salt Lake City: The Church of Jesus Christ of Latter-day Saints, 1932-51), 7:621.

9. Ibid., 7:622.

10. Thomas Bullock, Journals 1844-1850, 8 July 1848, LDS Church Archives.

11. An informative look at Angell's life and labors is found in Paul L. Anderson, "Truman O. Angell: Architect and Saint," in *Supporting Saints: Life Stories of Nineteenth-Century Mormons,* ed. Donald Q. Cannon and David J. Whittaker (Provo, Utah: Religious Studies Center, Brigham Young University, 1985), 133-74.

12. Truman O. Angell, Journal 1857-1868, 24 September 1867.

13. Ibid., 21 April 1868.

14. *Deseret News Weekly,* 19 April 1851.

15. Sermon of Brigham Young, delivered in the Carpenters' Hall in Salt Lake City, Utah, 16 December 1851, *JD* 1:376.

16. Truman O. Angell, Journal 1851-1856, 15 December 1851.

Chapter 3. "Beneath the Reach of Mountain Floods"

1. Printed on a Charles W. Carter photographic collage entitled "Salt Lake City Temple in its different stages of construction," LDS Church Archives.

2. Wilford Woodruff, Journals 1833-1898, 14 February 1853, LDS Church Archives.

3. John D. T. McAllister, Journals 1851-1906, 14 February 1853, LDS Church Archives. A typescript copy is available in the Special Collection Department, HBLLBYU.

4. Ibid.

5. JH, 14 February 1853.

6. John D. T. McAllister, Journals, 14 February 1853.

7. JH, 14 February 1853.

8. Wilford Woodruff, Journals, 14 February 1853.

9. JH, 14 February 1853.

10. Ibid.

11. John D. T. McAllister, Journals, 14 February 1853.

12. Wilford Woodruff, Journals, 14 February 1853.

13. John D. T. McAllister, Journals, 14 February 1853.

14. JH, 14 February 1853.

15. Wilford Woodruff, Journals, 15 February 1853.

16. Lorenzo Brown, Journals 1823-1893, 14 February 1853, HLSMC.

17. Printed on Carter photographic collage.

18. Wilford Woodruff, Journals, 22 February 1853.

19. Ibid., 1 March 1853.

20. Ibid., 19 March 1853.

21. Ibid., 24 March 1853.

22. Ibid., 4-5 April 1853.

23. JH, 14 February 1853.

24. *Deseret Evening News,* 16 April 1892.

25. Truman O. Angell, Journal 1851-1856, 17 March 1853.

26. *Illustrated London News,* 13 June 1857.

27. *Deseret Evening News,* 16 April 1892.

28. Ibid., 6 April 1892.

29. *Deseret News,* 6 April 1853.

30. Quoted in *House of the Lord* (1893), 7-8.

31. JH, 6 April 1853.

32. Lorenzo Brown, Journals, 6 April 1853.

33. JH, 6 April 1853.

34. Ibid.

35. Ibid.

36. Ibid.

37. *Deseret News,* 6 April 1853.

38. Ibid.

39. Ibid.

40. Ibid.

41. Ibid.

42. The First Presidency, *Ninth General Epistle of the Presidency of the Church of Jesus Christ of Latter-day Saints, from Great Salt Lake Valley, to the Saints scattered abroad throughout the Earth, Greetings* (Salt Lake City: First Presidency, 1853); also found in *Deseret News,* 13 April 1853.

43. Sermon of Brigham Young, delivered in the Old Tabernacle in Salt Lake City, Utah, 6 April 1853, *JD* 1:132.

44. Sermon of Parley P. Pratt, delivered in the Old Tabernacle in Salt Lake City, Utah, 7 April 1853, *JD* 1:14.

45. Joseph Curtis, Journal 1818-1881, 6 April 1853, HBLLBYU.

46. *Ninth General Epistle.*

47. Ibid.

48. *Deseret Evening News,* 12 October 1895.

49. *Millennial Star* 17 (28 April 1855): 266.

50. Charles Welcome Rockwood, Autobiography, LDS Church Archives.

Chapter 4. "Every Stone in It Is a Sermon"

1. In Conference Report, April 1915, 79.

2. Truman O. Angell, Journal 1851-1856, 3 April 1856.

3. *Harper's Weekly,* 11 July 1857.

4. Brigham Young, Journal 1857, 13 August 1857, Western American Collection, MLUU. A printed version is Everett L. Cooley, ed., *Diary of Brigham Young 1857* (Salt Lake City: University of Utah Library, 1980).

5. Wilford Woodruff, Journals 1833-1898, 13 August 1857, LDS Church Archives.

6. Ibid.

7. *Deseret News,* 23 September 1857.

8. Albert Tracy, Journal 1858-1860, 26 June 1858, New York Public Library, New York City, New York. A printed version is Cecil J. Allen and Robert J. Dwyer, eds., "The Utah Journal of Captain Albert Tracy, 1858-60," *Utah Historical Quarterly* 13 (1945); see also William Mulder and A. Russell Mortensen, eds., *Among the Mormons: Historic Accounts by Contemporary Observers* (New York: Alfred A. Knopf, 1969), 299-302.

9. Ibid.

10. Wilford Woodruff, Journals, 7 December 1859.

11. Sermon of Brigham Young, delivered in the Bowery in Salt Lake City, Utah, 6 October 1863, *JD* 10:254.

12. Charles Carter, Notebook, in private possession of Patricia Evans Baker, currently on loan to the Museum of Church History and Art, The Church of Jesus Christ of Latter-day Saints, Salt Lake City, Utah.

13. Annie Wells Cannon, "Passing Thoughts," *Woman's Exponent* (15 April and 1 May 1893): 157.

14. Joseph Fielding Smith, "The Salt Lake Temple," *Improvement Era* 56 (April 1953): 224.

15. "Two Utah Pioneers," in *Our Pioneer Heritage,* ed. Kate B. Carter, 20 vols. (Salt Lake City: Daughters of Utah Pioneers, 1964), 7:321.

16. Quoted in Gordon B. Hinckley, *James Henry Moyle* (Salt Lake City: Deseret Book Co., 1951), 80.

17. James H. Moyle, Journals 1879-1885, 29 November-10 December 1881, LDS Church Archives.

18. Benjamin T. Mitchell, Journal, in private possession of E. Lynn Dial, Salt Lake City, Utah.

19. Ibid.

20. Ibid.

21. Ibid.

22. B. H. Roberts, Autobiography, MLUU. A printed version is Gary James Bergera, ed., *The Autobiography of B. H. Roberts* (Salt Lake City: Signature Books, 1990).

23. Ibid.

24. *Deseret Weekly,* 16 April 1892.

25. Harry James Brown and Frederick D. Williams, eds., *The Diary of James A. Garfield,* 3 vols. (Lansing: Michigan State University Press, 1967), 2:75-76.

26. Frederic Trautmann, ed. and trans., "'Salt Lake City through a German's Eyes,' Theodor Kirchhoff in 1867," *Utah Historical Quarterly* 51 (Winter 1983): 48.

27. John Y. Simon, ed., *The Personal Memoirs of*

Julia Dent Grant (New York: G.P. Putnam's Sons, 1975), 185.

28. Ibid.

29. Edward W. Tullidge, *History of Salt Lake City and Its Founders* (Salt Lake City: n.p., 1881), 623.

30. Simon, *Personal Memoirs of Julia Grant*, 185.

31. *Saints' Herald*, 15 January 1877.

32. Governor Eli H. Murray to President Rutherford B. Hayes, 14 August 1880, Correspondences of President Hayes, Hayes Presidential Center, Spiegel Grove, Ohio.

33. *National Republican*, 6-7 September 1880.

34. Quoted in James P. Sharp, "Temple Recollections," *Improvement Era* 46 (April 1943): 199.

35. Ibid., 228.

36. *Deseret News*, 27 September 1878.

37. Brigham Young to Alfales Young, 17 August 1876, Brigham Young Collection, Letter Books, LDS Church Archives; all cited Brigham Young correspondences are located in this collection. A printed version of Brigham Young correspondences to his sons is Dean C. Jessee, ed., *Letters of Brigham Young to His Sons* (Salt Lake City: Deseret Book, 1974).

38. JH, 6 April 1876.

39. Wilford Woodruff, Journals, 22 May 1876.

40. First Presidency, *To the Bishops, Seventies, High Priests and Elders,* (Fall 1876), LDS Church Archives.

41. Ibid.

42. A brief history of early Utah Latter-day Saint temples, including historic photographs, can be found in Steven L. Olson, *Nineteenth-Century Utah Temples* (Salt Lake City: Museum of Church History and Art, The Church of Jesus Christ of Latter-day Saints, 1984); for a review of the entire history of temple building among the Latter-day Saints, both in the nineteenth and twentieth centuries, see Richard O. Cowan, *Temples to Dot the Earth* (Salt Lake City: Bookcraft, 1989).

43. Brigham Young to John Willard Young, 26 October 1874.

44. Brigham Young to Ward E. Pack, 23 May 1877.

45. Many Latter-day Saints also believed that April was the month of Jesus Christ's birth, instead of the Christmas date assigned through tradition.

46. *Deseret Evening News,* 3 October 1881.

47. Gwennie Starley Matheson, comp., John Starley, Gardener and Foreman of the Salt Lake Temple Block, USHS.

48. "The Memoirs of President Joseph Smith (1832-1914)," *Saints' Herald,* 25 February 1936.

49. *Deseret Evening News,* 31 October 1885.

50. A discussion of this period of Utah history is found in Edward Leo Lyman, *Political Deliverance: The Mormon Quest for Utah Statehood* (Urbana: University of Illinois Press, 1986).

Chapter 5. "I Want to See the . . . Temple Finished"

1. Wilford Woodruff, Journals 1833-1898, 9 October 1887, LDS Church Archives.

2. Quoted in Laura P. Angell King, "Truman O. Angell, Sr.," in *Heart Throbs of the West,* ed. Kate B. Carter, 12 vols. (Salt Lake City: Daughters of Utah Pioneers, 1941), 3:71.

3. Wilford Woodruff, Journals, 3 December 1888.

4. Ibid., 4 July 1889.

5. Ibid., 23 May 1890.

6. Ibid., 25 September 1890.

7. *Deseret Evening News,* 9 May 1891.

8. JH, 9 May 1891.

9. Abraham H. Cannon, Journals 1879-1895, 7 October 1891, Manuscript Division, HBLLBYU.

10. *Millennial Star* 52 (24 February 1890): 128.

11. Abraham H. Cannon, Journals, 27 August 1891.

12. An illustrated history of this mission is found in Linda Jones Gibbs, *Harvesting the Light: The Paris Art Mission and Beginnings of Utah Impressionism* (Salt Lake City: Museum of Church History and Art, The Church of Jesus Christ of Latter-day Saints, 1987); see also Martha Elizabeth Bradley and Lowell M. Durham, Jr., "John Hafen and the Art Missionaries," *Journal of Mormon History* 12 (1985): 91-105.

13. John B. Fairbanks, Diary June-July 1890, 24 June 1890, Manuscript Division, HBLLBYU.

14. Ibid.

15. George Q. Cannon to Lorus Pratt, 12 September 1891, in private possession of Mr. and Mrs. David Glover, quoted in Gibbs, *Harvesting the Light,* 31-32.

16. Abraham H. Cannon, Journals, 13 July 1891.

17. Ibid., 10 April 1892.

18. Joseph Henry Dean, Journals 1876-1944, 5 February 1892, LDS Church Archives.

19. Henry Charles Barrell, 1846-1908, "The Fulfillment of a Dream, 1892," LDS Church Archives.

20. Ibid.

21. Ibid.

22. Wilford Woodruff, Journals, 29 March 1892.

23. Ibid., Journals, 16 March 1892.

Chapter 6. "The Greatest Day the Latter-day Saints Ever Saw"

1. Abraham H. Cannon, Journals 1879-1895, 17 March 1892, Manuscript Division, HBLLBYU.

2. *Deseret Evening News,* 5 April 1892.

3. Marriner Wood Merrill, Journals 1832-1906, 2 April 1892, LDS Church Archives. Extracts from Merrill's journals are found in Melvin Clarence Merrill, ed., *Utah Pioneer and Apostle Marriner Wood Merrill and His Family* (Salt Lake City: n.p., 1937).

4. Charles Lowell Walker, Diaries 1854-1904, 1 April 1892, LDS Church Archives. A printed version of these diaries is A. Karl Larson and Katharine Miles Larson, ed., *Diary of Charles Lowell Walker* (Logan, Utah: Utah State University Press, 1980).

5. James E. Talmage, Diaries 1876-1933, 5 April 1892, Manuscript Division, HBLLBYU.

6. Abraham H. Cannon, Journals, 4 April 1892.

7. Jesse W. Crosby, Diaries 1884-1914, 5 April 1892, HLSMC.

8. *Deseret Evening News,* 6 April 1892.

9. Joseph Henry Dean, Journals 1876-1944, 6 April 1892, LDS Church Archives.

10. Abraham H. Cannon, Journals, 6 April 1892.

11. *Deseret Evening News,* 6 April 1892.

12. Quoted in Thomas C. Romney, *The Life of Lorenzo Snow* (Salt Lake City: Sugarhouse Press, 1955), 470.

13. B. H. Roberts, *A Comprehensive History of The Church of Jesus Christ of Latter-day Saints,* 6 vols. (Salt Lake City: The Church of Jesus Christ of Latter-day Saints, 1930), 3:317.

14. Charles Lowell Walker, Diaries, 6 April 1892.

15. Joseph Henry Dean, Journals, 6 April 1892.

16. JH, 6 April 1893.

17. Ibid.

18. "Autobiography of John Lingren," in *Treasures of Pioneer History,* ed. Kate B. Carter, 6 vols. (Salt Lake City: Daughters of Utah Pioneers, 1952), 1:261.

19. *House of the Lord* (1893), 12.

20. James E. Talmage, Diaries, 6 April 1892.

21. Emmeline B. Wells, Journals 1875-1909, 6 April 1892, HBLLBYU.

22. H. W. Naisbitt, "Temple Building," *Contributor* 13 (April 1892): 258.

23. "Autobiography of John Lingren," 261.

24. Joseph Henry Dean, Journals, 6 April 1892.

25. Ibid.

26. Charles Roscoe Savage, Journals 1855-1909, 6 April 1892, Manuscript Division, HBLLBYU.

27. *Deseret Evening News,* 6 April 1892.

28. Joseph Henry Dean, Journals, 6 April 1892.

29. Mary Ann Burnham Freeze, Diaries, 6 April 1892, HBLLBYU.

30. Susa Young Gates, "Temple Workers," *Young Woman's Journal* 4 (April 1893): 304.

31. Abraham H. Cannon, Journals, 6 April 1892; Joseph Henry Dean, Journals, 6 April 1892.

32. Leonard John Nuttall, Diaries 1876-1904, 6 April 1892, HBLLBYU. A typescript of these diaries is located in the Special Collection Department, HBLLBYU.

33. *Deseret Evening News,* 6 April 1892.

34. William Y. Jeffs, Journals 1886-1893, in private possession of Donald R. Jeffs, Salt Lake City, Utah.

35. Quoted in Rell G. Francis, *Cyrus E. Dallin: Let Justice Be Done* (Springville: Springville Museum of Art, 1976), 66.

36. Ibid., 68.

37. Incandescent bulbs were used to light the exterior of the building until flood lamps replaced them, beginning on 6 April 1930 during the Church's centennial celebration.

38. Jane Wilkie Hooper Blood, Diaries 1880-1898, 7 April 1892, LDS Church Archives.

39. Emmeline B. Wells, Journals, 7 April 1892.

40. Wilford Woodruff, Journals, 6 April 1892.

41. Leonard John Nuttall, Diaries, 7 April 1892.

42. Color photographs of these windows are found in Joyce Athay Janetski, "Louis Comfort Tiffany: Stained Glass in Utah," *Utah Preservation/Restoration: A Publication for the Preservationist* 3 (1981): 20-25.

Chapter 7. "That . . . We May All Be Found Acceptable"

1. Wilford Woodruff, Journals 1833-1898, 11 April 1892, LDS Church Archives.

2. Abraham H. Cannon, Journals 1879-1895, 15 April 1892, Manuscript Division, HBLLBYU.

3. Wilford Woodruff, George Q. Cannon, and Joseph F. Smith to John Clawson, Lorus Pratt, John B. Fairbanks, Edwin Evans, and Herman Haag, 18 April 1892, First Presidency Collection, Letter Books, LDS Church Archives.

4. Samuel Richards, Journals 1839-1909, 22 April 1892, LDS Church Archives.

5. Ibid., 20 May 1892.

6. Ibid., 12 September 1892.

7. Marriner Wood Merrill, Journals 1832-1906, 1 May 1892, LDS Church Archives.

8. Abraham H. Cannon, Journals, 1 May 1892.

9. Ibid.

10. Ibid., 4 August 1892.

11. Wilford Woodruff, Journals, 4 August 1892.

12. Abraham H. Cannon, Journals, 4 August 1892.

13. Leonard John Nuttall, Diaries 1876-1904, 7 October 1892, HBLLBYU.

14. Samuel Richards, Journals, 7 October 1892.

15. Leonard John Nuttall, Diaries, 10 October 1892.

16. Abraham H. Cannon, Journals, 10 October 1892.

17. Joseph Don Carlos Young to Dan Weggeland, 21 October 1892, Joseph Don Carlos Young Collection, LDS Church Archives.

18. Wilford Woodruff, Journals, 12 January 1893.

19. James H. Anderson, "The Salt Lake Temple," *Contributor* 14 (April 1893): 288-89, 291.

20. Samuel Richards, Journals, 24 November 1892.

21. Abraham H. Cannon, Journals, 21 December 1892.

22. Heber J. Grant to John C. Sharp, 1 January 1893, Heber J. Grant Collection, Letter Books, LDS Church Archives.

23. Wilford Woodruff, Journals, 3 January 1893.

24. Ibid., 25 January 1893.

25. Ibid., 30 January 1893.

26. Abraham H. Cannon, Journals, 21 March 1893.

27. Wilford Woodruff, Journals, 18 March 1893.

28. Quoted in Joseph Heinerman, *Temple Manifestations* (Salt Lake City: Magazine Printing and Publishing, 1974), 128-29.

29. Wilford Woodruff, Journals, 17 March 1893.

30. *Dedication of the Mormon Temple, Salt Lake City, Utah, April 6th, 1893* (St. Louis: Woodward & Tiernan Printing Co., 1893).

31. First Presidency, *An Address to the Officers and Members of the Church of Jesus Christ of Latter-day Saints* (Salt Lake City: The Church of Jesus Christ of Latter-day Saints, First Presidency, March 1893), 1; see also James R. Clark, ed., *Messages of the First Presidency,* 6 vols. (Salt Lake City: Bookcraft, 1965-1975), 3:241-44.

32. Ibid.

33. Ibid.

34. Marriner Wood Merrill, Journals, 23 March 1893.

35. Henry Ballard, Private Journal of Henry Ballard, 25 March 1893, HLSMC.

36. Mary Ann Burnham Freeze, Diaries, 25 March 1893, HBLLBYU.

37. Wilford Woodruff, Journals, 25 March 1893.

38. B. H. Roberts, Journal, 30 March 1893, in pri-vate possession, quoted in Truman G. Madsen, *Defender of the Faith: The B. H. Roberts Story* (Salt Lake City: Bookcraft, 1980), 210.

39. Wilford Woodruff, Journals, 30 March 1893.

40. Lelia Westwood, "Etiquette," *Young Woman's Journal* 4 (April 1893): 322.

41. Ibid.

42. "Preparations for the Dedication," *Contributor* 14 (March 1893): 235.

Chapter 8. "Members of the Church . . . Are Cordially Invited"

1. *Deseret Weekly,* 1 April 1893.

2. David John, Journals 1833-1908, 3 April 1893, Manuscript Division, HBLLBYU.

3. Quoted in the *Los Angeles Times,* 6 April 1893.

4. Jesse Nathaniel Smith, Autobiography and Journals 1855-1906, 31 March 1893, LDS Church Archives. A printed version is Oliver R. Smith, ed., *Six Decades in the Early West: The Journal of Jesse Nathaniel Smith,* 3rd ed. (Provo: Jesse N. Smith Assn., 1970).

5. Ibid.

6. Benjamin F. Johnson, *My Life's Review* (n.p., n.d.), 377.

7. Ibid.

8. *Deseret Evening News,* 5 April 1893.

9. Abraham H. Cannon, Journals 1879-1895, 19 May 1893, Manuscript Division, HBLLBYU.

10. Lucy Flake, Autobiography and Diary of Lucy Hannah White Flake, typescript, Special Collections, HBLLBYU; extracts from Flake's autobiography and diary are found in Lucy Hannah White Flake, *To the Last Frontier: Autobiography of Lucy Hannah White Flake* (Mesa: Roberta Flake Clayton, 1976).

11. Ibid.

12. Ibid.

13. "Young Folks' Stories," *Juvenile Instructor* 28 (15 April 1893): 362.

14. *Deseret Evening News,* 4 April 1893.

15. James E. Talmage, Diaries 1876-1933, 6 April 1893, Manuscript Division, HBLLBYU.

16. *Deseret Evening News,* 10 April 1893.

17. Lorenzo Brown, Journals 1823-1893, 21-22 September 1892, HLSMC.

18. A discussion of this change is found in Thomas G. Alexander and James B. Allen, *Mormons and Gentiles: A History of Salt Lake City* (Boulder: Pruett Publishing Co., 1984), 87-130.

19. JH, 29 December 1890.

20. *Deseret Evening News,* 4 April 1893.

21. Ibid., 6 April 1893.

22. Ibid., 7 April 1893.

23. JH, 30 March 1893.

24. *Deseret Evening News,* 8 April 1893.

25. Ibid., 7 April 1893.

26. Abraham H. Cannon, Journals, 2 April 1893.

27. Leonard John Nuttall, Diaries 1876-1904, 1 April 1893, HBLLBYU.

28. *Deseret Evening News,* 5 April 1893.

29. Ibid.

30. B. H. Roberts, Journal, 22 April 1893, in private possession.

31. JH, 5 April 1893.

32. Sermon of George Q. Cannon, delivered in the New Tabernacle in Salt Lake City, Utah, 8 April 1871, *JD* 14:125.

33. "Topics of the Times," *Juvenile Instructor* 28 (15 April 1893): 286.

34. Joseph Henry Dean, Journals 1876-1944, 5 April 1893, LDS Church Archives.

35. *Salt Lake Herald,* 7 April 1893.

36. *Salt Lake Tribune,* 6 April 1893.

37. Ibid.

38. Interview published in the *Deseret Evening News,* 6 April 1893.

39. Ibid.

40. *Deseret Evening News,* 5 April 1893.

41. Emmeline B. Wells, "Temple Dedication," *Woman's Exponent* (15 April and 1 May 1893): 156.

42. Ibid.

43. Wilford Woodruff, Journals 1833-1898, 4 April 1893, LDS Church Archives.

44. Lucy Flake, Autobiography and Diary.

45. Leonard John Nuttall, Diaries, 4 April 1893.

46. *Deseret Evening News,* 5 April 1893.

Chapter 9. "The Spirit of God Filled the House"

1. Charles Lowell Walker, Diaries 1854-1904, 6 April 1893, LDS Church Archives.

2. *Deseret Evening News,* 6 April 1893.

3. Lucy Flake, Autobiography and Diary of Lucy Hannah White Flake, typescript, Special Collections, HBLLBYU.

4. Joseph Henry Dean, Journals 1876-1944, 6 April 1893, LDS Church Archives.

5. Benjamin F. Johnson, *My Life's Review* (n.p. n.d.), 378.

6. Ibid.

7. Joseph Henry Dean, Journals, 6 April 1893.

8. Thomas Scott Griggs, Diaries 1861-1903, 6 April 1893, LDS Church Archives.

9. Heber Bennion, Journals 1882-1931, 6 April 1893, HLSMC.

10. "Editorial Thoughts," *Juvenile Instructor* 28 (15 April 1893): 219.

11. First Presidency, *An Address to the Officers and Members of the Church of Jesus Christ of Latter-day Saints* (Salt Lake City: The Church of Jesus Christ of Latter-day Saints, First Presidency, March 1893), 1.

12. *Deseret Evening News,* 5 April 1893.

13. *Salt Lake Herald,* 7 April 1893.

14. John D. T. McAllister, Journals 1851-1906, 6 April 1893, LDS Church Archives.

15. Annie Wells Cannon, "Passing Thoughts," *Woman's Exponent* (15 April and 1 May 1893): 157.

16. Charles Roscoe Savage, Journals 1855-1909, 6 April 1893, Manuscript Division, HBLLBYU.

17. Bardella Shipp Curtis, Autobiography 1874-1957, LDS Church Archives.

18. Francis Asbury Hammond, Journals 1852-1893, 6 April 1893, LDS Church Archives.

19. Ibid.

20. Emmeline B. Wells, "Temple Dedication," *Woman's Exponent* (15 April and 1 May 1893): 156.

21. Leonard John Nuttall, Diaries 1876-1904, 6 April 1893, HBLLBYU.

22. Thomas Scott Griggs, Diaries, 6 April 1893.

23. Joseph Henry Dean, Journals, 6 April 1893.

24. Amy Brown, Lyman, *In Retrospect: Autobiography of Amy Brown Lyman* (Salt Lake City: General Board of Relief Society, 1945), 23.

25. *Deseret Evening News,* 6 April 1893.

26. Ibid.

27. Ibid.

28. Rudger Clawson, Journal 1 May 1891 to 21 December 1905, 6 April 1893, MLUU.

29. John Henry Smith, Diaries 1875-1911, 6 April 1893, MLUU. A printed version is Jean Bickmore White, ed., *Church, State, and Politics: The Diaries of John Henry Smith* (Salt Lake City: Signature Books, 1990).

30. Francis M. Lyman, Journal, typescript, 17 April 1893, in private possession of Leo Lyman, Spring Valley Lake, California; original journal in LDS Church Archives.

31. David John, Journals 1833-1908, 6 April 1893, Manuscript Division, HBLLBYU.

32. Wilford Woodruff, Journals 1833-1898, 31 December 1893, LDS Church Archives.

33. Andrew Jenson, Diaries 1864-1941, 6 April 1893, LDS Church Archives.

34. Leonard John Nuttall, Diaries, 6 April 1893.

35. James L. Bunting, Journals 1857-1920, 23 April 1893, HBLLBYU.

36. *Deseret Evening News,* 6 April 1893.

37. Andrew Jenson, Diaries, 7 April 1893.

38. Rudger Clawson, Journal, 6 April 1893.

39. *Los Angeles Times,* 7 April 1893.

40. Samuel Richards, Journals 1839-1909, 6 April 1893, LDS Church Archives.

41. Joseph Fielding Smith, "The Salt Lake Temple," *Improvement Era* 56 (April 1953): 224.

42. Wilford Woodruff, Journals, 6 April 1893.

43. Heber Bennion, Journals, 6 April 1893.

44. Lucy Flake, Autobiography and Diary.

45. Francis Asbury Hammond, Journals, 6 April 1893.

46. Annie Wells Cannon, "Passing Thoughts," 157.

47. Francis Asbury Hammond, Journals, 6 April 1893.

48. Jane Wilkie Hooper Blood, Diaries 1880-1898, 6 April 1893, LDS Church Archives.

49. *Deseret News Weekly,* 6 May 1893.

50. Mary Ann Burnham Freeze, Diaries, 6 April 1893, HBLLBYU.

51. Joseph Henry Dean, Journals, 10 April 1893.

52. *San Francisco Chronicle,* 7 April 1893.

53. Many large city newspapers had reporters present for the occasion, while other newspapers relied on the news services or reports from other newspapers. The RLDS Church's *Saints' Herald* published a short one-column news story based on the Chicago *Record,* "whose correspondent at Salt Lake City wrote up the matter" (see the *Saints' Herald,* 6 May 1893).

54. *Los Angeles Times,* 7 April 1893.

55. *Constitution-Democrat,* 17 May 1893.

56. Quoted in the *Deseret Weekly,* 27 May 1893.

57. George F. Richards, Diaries 1880-1950, 7 April 1893, LDS Church Archives.

58. Alice Minerva Richards Tate Robinson, Book of Remembrance, in private possession of George F. Tate, Orem, Utah.

59. Alice Minerva Richards [Tate Robinson], Personal Record, in private possession of George F. Tate, Orem, Utah.

60. Thomas Sleight, Diaries, 7 April 1893, LDS Church Archives.

61. Ibid.

62. Ibid.

63. James L. Bunting, Journals, 7 April 1893.

64. *Chicago Tribune,* 7 April 1893.

65. Lucy Flake, Autobiography and Diary.

66. James E. Talmage, Diaries 1876-1933, 9 April 1893, Manuscript Division, HBLLBYU.

67. Leonard John Nuttall, Diaries, 11 April 1893.

68. Francis M. Lyman, Journal, 17 April 1893.

69. Rudger Clawson, Journal, 19 April 1893.

70. B. H. Roberts, Journal, 19 April 1893, in private possession.

71. Marriner Wood Merrill, Journals 1832-1906, 19 April 1893, LDS Church Archives.

72. Ibid., 20 April 1893.

73. Rudger Clawson, Journal, 20 April 1893.

74. Leonard John Nuttall, Diaries, 20 April 1893. Although the use of water instead of wine in the sacrament comes clearly within the authorization in Doctrine and Covenants 27:2, the use of pure wine prepared by the Saints was not completely and officially abandoned until 1906.

75. B. H. Roberts, Journal, 20 April 1893.

76. Francis Asbury Hammond, Journals, 20 April 1893.

77. Rudger Clawson, Journal, 20 April 1893.

78. Leonard John Nuttall, Diaries, 20 April 1893.

79. Ibid.

80. Ibid.

81. James L. Bunting, Journals, 28 April 1893.

82. George F. Richards, Diaries, 22 April 1893.

83. LeGrand Richards, Personal Oral History Interview, in private possession of George F. Tate, Orem, Utah. More than eighty years later in 1978, however, LeGrand saw a heavenly personage in the temple. He told his children and grandchildren he had seen Wilford Woodruff while attending a meeting in the Council of the Twelve Room in the Salt Lake Temple. Personal interview with family members, 18 November 1991.

84. Emmeline B. Wells, "Temple Dedication," 156.

85. Jane Wilkie Hooper Blood, Diaries, 21 April 1893.

86. Emmeline B. Wells, "Temple Dedication," 154.

87. Jesse Nathaniel Smith, Autobiography and Journals 1855-1906, 6 April 1893, LDS Church Archives.

88. "Extracts from a sermon by President Woodruff," typescript in private possession of Leo Lyman, Spring Valley Lake, California; original in Wilford Woodruff Papers, Wilford Woodruff Collection, LDS Church Archives; see also "Official Declaration—1, Excerpts from Three Addresses by President Wilford Woodruff Regarding the Manifesto," in Doctrine and

Covenants (Salt Lake City: The Church of Jesus Christ of Latter-day Saints, 1981), 293.

89. Wilford Woodruff, Journals, 31 December 1893.

90. John Henry Smith, Diaries, 7 April 1893.

91. Jesse Nathaniel Smith, Journals, 8 April 1893.

92. Abraham H. Cannon, Journals 1879-1895, 18 May 1893, Manuscript Division, HBLLBYU.

93. "Temple Manifestations: The Salt Lake Temple," *Contributor* 16 (December 1894): 117.

94. Rudger Clawson, Journal, 8 April 1893.

95. "Temple Manifestations: The Salt Lake Temple," 117-18.

96. Hans Jensen Hals, Journal 1829-1910, 6 April 1893, LDS Church Archives.

97. Rudger Clawson, Journal, 10 April 1893.

98. Francil M. Lyman, Journal, 17 April 1893.

99. *Deseret Evening News,* 6 April 1893.

100. "Temple Manifestations: The Salt Lake Temple," 118.

101. Jesse Nathaniel Smith, Journals, 8 April 1893.

102. Annie Wells Cannon, "Passing Thoughts," 157.

103. JH, 6 April 1893.

104. Annie Wells Cannon, "Passing Thoughts," 157.

105. John Henry Smith, Diaries, 7 April 1893.

106. James E. Talmage, Diaries, 7 April 1893.

107. Joseph B. Keeler, "A Wonderful Manifestation," *Juvenile Instructor* 32 (1 January 1897): 34-36.

108. Leonard John Nuttall, Diaries, 7 April 1893.

109. Jesse Nathaniel Smith, Journals, 19 April 1893.

110. Lucy Flake, Autobiography and Diary.

111. Ibid.

112. Jesse Nathaniel Smith, Journals, 7 May 1893.

113. Henry Ballard, Private Journal of Henry Ballard, 8 April 1893, HLSMC.

114. Levi Savage Jr., Journal 1851-1935, 19 April 1893, USHS.

115. Eliza S. Keeler, Journals 1840-1893, April 1893, HBLLBYU.

116. Wilford Woodruff, Journals, 31 May 1893.

117. Leonard John Nuttall, Diaries, 21 April 1893.

118. Ibid., 22 April 1893.

119. Ibid., 7 May 1893.

120. A detailed study of these events is found in Thomas G. Alexander, *Things in Heaven and Earth: The Life and Times of Wilford Woodruff, a Mormon Prophet* (Salt Lake City: Signature Books, 1991), 290-96.

121. Wilford Woodruff, Journals, 31 December 1893.

122. Ibid.

Chapter 10. "I Have a Mission for You to Fill"

1. Susa Young Gates, "Temple Workers," *Young Woman's Journal* 4 (April 1893): 300.

2. Susa Young Gates, "The Temple Workers' Excursion," *Young Woman's Journal* 5 (August 1894): 515.

3. Susa Young Gates, "Temple Workers," 294.

4. Joseph Henry Dean, Journals 1876-1944, 2 May 1893, LDS Church Archives.

5. Ibid.

6. "Life and Ancestry of Joseph Christenson," *Utah Genealogical and Historical Magazine* 28 (October 1937): 148.

7. Sarah Josephine Clausen Jensen, Mormon Biographical Collection, LDS Church Archives.

8. Leonard John Nuttall, Diaries 1876-1904, 6 May 1893, HBBLLBYU.

9. Mary Ann Burnham Freeze, Diaries, 6 May 1893, HBLLBYU.

10. Lorenzo Snow, Letters 1893-94, 9 May 1893, HBLLBYU.

11. John D. T. McAllister, Journals 1851-1906, 16 May 1893, LDS Church Archives.

12. Leonard John Nuttall, Diaries, 16 May 1893.

13. Salt Lake Temple Historical Record 1893-1918, Salt Lake Temple Collection, LDS Church Archives.

14. Ibid.

15. Abraham H. Cannon, Journals 1879-1895, 20 May 1893, Manuscript Division, HBLLBYU.

16. Leonard John Nuttall, Diaries, 24 May 1893.

17. According to Lucy Flake, she and her husband had two children adopted to them in the temple on 7 April 1893. Joseph F. Smith reportedly said on that occasion, "Your names will go down on the great record as the first work in this new temple." Lucy Flake, Autobiography and Diary of Lucy Hannah White Flake, typescript, Special Collections, HBLLBYU.

18. Leonard John Nuttall, Diaries, 1 June 1893.

19. Abraham H. Cannon, Journals, 25 May 1893.

20. Wilford Woodruff, Journals 1833-1898, 23 June 1893, LDS Church Archives.

21. Abraham H. Cannon, Journals, 23 June 1893.

22. Ibid.

23. Ibid., 13 July 1893.

24. Salt Lake Temple, Minutes of a Special Meeting of Sister Workers, 6 July 1893, Salt Lake Temple Collection, LDS Church Archives.

25. Susa Young Gates, *History of the Young Ladies' Mutual Improvement Association* (Salt Lake City: Deseret News Press, 1911), 26-28.

26. Emmeline B. Wells, "Temple Dedication," *Woman's Exponent* (15 April and 1 May 1893): 156.

Epilogue

1. Joseph Fielding Smith, "The Salt Lake Temple," *Improvement Era* 56 (April 1953): 224.

2. Annie Wells Cannon, "Passing Thoughts," *Woman's Exponent* (15 April and 1 May 1893): 157.

3. Sermon of Brigham Young, delivered in the Bowery in Salt Lake City, Utah, 6 October 1863, *JD* 10:252.

4. "A Great Temple," *Juvenile Instructor* 28 (15 April 1893): 242.

5. B. H. Roberts, Journal, 24 April 1893, in private possession.

6. Samuel Lorenzo Adams, manuscript dated 6 April 1893, LDS Church Archives.

Appendix: The Design of the Salt Lake Temple

1. The most detailed history written to date on the construction of the Salt Lake Temple is W. A. Raynor, *The Everlasting Spires: A Story of the Salt Lake Temple* (Salt Lake City: Deseret Book Co., 1965). Another classic work is James E. Talmage, *The House of the Lord* (Salt Lake City: Bookcraft, 1962), originally published in 1912. This book contains a detailed description of the temple interior and the full text of President Woodruff's dedication prayer. Information regarding the historical context of Talmage's publication effort, which included the first interior photographs of the temple, is found in Gary James Bergera, "'I'm here for the cash': Max Florence and the Great Mormon Temple," *Utah Historical Quarterly* 47 (Winter 1979): 54-63.

2. *New York Times,* 7 April 1893.

3. *Salt Lake Herald,* 7 April 1893.

4. For a discussion of the architectural history of the Salt Lake Temple, see C. Mark Hamilton, *The Salt Lake Temple: A Monument to a People* (Salt Lake City:

University Services, Incorporated, 1983). C. Mark Hamilton, "The Salt Lake Temple: A Symbolic Statement of Mormon Doctrine," in *The Mormon People: Their Character and Traditions,* ed. Thomas G. Alexander (Provo, Utah: Brigham Young University Press, 1980), 103-27, interprets the symbolism of the exterior portion of the temple.

5. *Deseret News,* 17 August 1854.

6. *Deseret Weekly,* 9 April 1892.

7. *Chicago Tribune,* 7 April 1893.

8. *San Francisco Chronicle,* 7 April 1893.

9. Interview with Randall Dixon (LDS Church Historical Department) and Steven Epperson (LDS Museum of Church History and Art) on 15 November 1991. During the 1991 restoration project at the temple, workers removed the white paint from these two stones and found flecks of flesh-colored paint on the hands of the "handclasp" stone and blue on the eye and curtain of the "all-seeing eye" stone.

10. *Deseret News,* 17 August 1854.

11. James H. Anderson, "The Salt Lake Temple," *Contributor* 14 (April 1893): 275.

12. W. H. Folsom to John Taylor, 24 May 1878, John Taylor Collection, LDS Church Archives.

13. James L. Bunting, Journals 1857-1920, 6 April 1893, HBLLBYU.

14. Henry Ballard, Private Journal of Henry Ballard, 6 April 1893, HLSMC.

15. Talmage, *House of the Lord,* 100.

16. *Salt Lake Herald,* 7 April 1893.

17. Marriner Wood Merrill, Journals 1832-1906, 11 April 1893, LDS Church Archives.

18. *Deseret Weekly,* 1 April 1893.

19. Ibid., 16 April 1892.

20. Leonard John Nuttall, Diaries 1876-1904, 23 April 1893, HBLLBYU.

21. *House of the Lord* (1893), 23.

22. Quoted in Albert L. Zobell, Jr., and Edward O. Anderson, "Salt Lake Temple," *Improvement Era* 68 (August 1965): 687.

23. Andrew Jenson, Diaries 1864-1941, 6 April 1893, LDS Church Archives.

24. *San Francisco Chronicle,* 7 April 1893.

25. In Conference Report, October 1928, 86.

Photographic Sources

The abbreviations listed below have been used to simplify references in the photographic sources that follow:

HBLLBYU — Photoarchives, Harold B. Lee Library, Brigham Young University, Provo, Utah

LDS Church Archives — Archives Division, Church Historical Department, The Church of Jesus Christ of Latter-day Saints, Salt Lake City, Utah; all photographs from LDS Church Archives are used with permission

LDSVRL — Visual Resources Library, The Church of Jesus Christ of Latter-day Saints, Salt Lake City, Utah

MCHA — Museum of Church History and Art, The Church of Jesus Christ of Latter-day Saints, Salt Lake City, Utah; all photographs from MCHA are used with permission

USHS — Utah State Historical Society, Salt Lake City, Utah

In the photographic sources below, the page number on which a photograph appears is followed by date, photographer, collection name, and repository.

Frontispiece
Page ii.   Ronald Read, MCHA.

Chapter 1. "God Gathers Together His People in the Last Days"
Page xii. Ca. 1880, HBLLBYU.

Chapter 2. "Here We Shall Build a Temple to Our God"
Page 4.   Ca. 1850, LDS Church Archives.

Chapter 3. "Beneath the Reach of Mountain Floods"
Page 8.   14 February 1853, William A. Smith, Daguerreotype Collection, LDS Church Archives.
Page 12. LDS Church Archives.

Page 15. 1853, Frederick Piercy engraving in Linforth, *Route from Liverpool to Great Salt Lake Valley* (1855), in private possession, Edward W. Griffith Mormon Americana Collection, Irvine, California.

Chapter 4. "Every Stone in It Is a Sermon"
Page 16. Ca. 1874, Charles William Carter, Salt Lake Temple File, USHS.
Page 18. In private possession, Greg Christofferson Mormon Americana Collection, Irvine, California.
Page 21. 1873, Charles Roscoe Savage, LDS Church Archives.
Page 22. Ca. 1874, Charles William Carter, LDS Church Archives.
Page 25 (top). 1875, Charles William Carter, HBLLBYU.
Page 25 (middle). Ca. 1879, Salt Lake Temple File, USHS.
Page 25 (bottom). Ca. 1879, LDS Church Archives.
Page 26. Ca. 1886, Charles Ellis Johnson, Charles Ellis Johnson Collection, HBLLBYU.
Page 28. Ca. 1885, Alexander Martin, LDS Church Archives.
Page 30. 1886, LDS Church Archives.

Chapter 5. "I Want to See the . . . Temple Finished"

Page 32. Ca. 1891, Charles Ellis Johnson, Charles Ellis Johnson Collection, HBLLBYU.

Page 34. Ca. 1890, LDS Church Archives.

Page 36. Ca. 1890, Springville Museum of Art, Springville, Utah.

Page 37. Ca. 1890, LDS Church Archives.

Page 38. 1892, LDS Church Archives.

Chapter 6. "The Greatest Day the Latter-day Saints Ever Saw"

Page 40. 6 April 1892, C. L. Joy, LDS Church Archives.

Page 42. 6 April 1892, Salt Lake Temple File, USHS.

Page 44. LDS Church Archives.

Page 45. 6 April 1892, LDS Church Archives.

Page 46. 6 April 1892, Charles Ellis Johnson, Charles Ellis Johnson Collection, HBLLBYU.

Page 47. HBLLBYU.

Page 48. 1892, Salt Lake Temple File, USHS.

Page 49. 6 April 1892, Charles Roscoe Savage, LDS Church Archives.

Chapter 7. "That . . . We May All Be Found Acceptable"

Page 50. LDS Church Archives.

Page 52. 1892, John Olsen, LDS Church Archives.

Page 53. Ronald Read, MCHA.

Page 55. Ca. 1892, LDS Church Archives.

Chapter 8. "Members of the Church . . . Are Cordially Invited"

Page 58. 1893, James H. Crockwell, LDS Church Archives.

Page 63. 1911, Ralph Savage, C. R. Savage Company, LDS Church Archives.

Chapter 9. "The Spirit of God Filled the House"

Page 66. 6 April 1893, Charles Ellis Johnson, Charles Ellis Johnson Collection, HBLLBYU.

Page 68. 6 April 1893, George Edward Anderson, George Edward Anderson Collection, HBLLBYU.

Page 70. In private possession, Greg Christofferson Mormon Americana Collection, Irvine, California.

Page 72. Western Americana, J. Willard Marriott Library, University of Utah, Salt Lake City, Utah.

Page 73. In private possession, R. Q. Shupe Mormon Americana Collection, San Juan Capistrano, California.

Page 75. LDS Church Archives.

Page 77. Jed Clark, MCHA.

Page 79. 1911, Ralph Savage, C. R. Savage Company, LDS Church Archives.

Page 84. 6 April 1893, Charles Ellis Johnson, LDS Church Archives.

Chapter 10. "I Have a Mission for You to Fill"

Page 86. 1893, Salt Lake Temple File, USHS.

Page 89 (top left). Ca. 1893, Charles William Carter, Charles William Carter Collection, LDS Church Archives.

Page 89 (bottom right). Ca. 1893, Laurence Wilson copy, Portrait Collection, LDS Church Archives.

Page 90. Ca. 1885, LDS Church Archives.

Epilogue

Page 92. Ca. 1893, Charles Ellis Johnson, Charles Ellis Johnson Collection, HBLLBYU.

Page 94. Ca. 1896, LDS Church Archives.

Appendix: The Design of the Salt Lake Temple

Page 96. 1940, W. Lincoln Highton, Federal Works Agency Collection, Small Prints Division, United States National Archives, Washington, D.C.

Page 100 (top left). LDSVRL.

Page 100 (top right). Ronald Read, MCHA.

Page 100 (bottom). LDSVRL.

Page 101. 1911, Ralph Savage, C. R. Savage Company, LDS Church Archives.

Page 102. 1911, Ralph Savage, C. R. Savage Company, LDS Church Archives.

Back Cover

Top. Ca. 1879, Salt Lake Temple File, USHS.

Middle. Ca. 1890, Charles Roscoe Savage, LDS Church Archives.

Bottom. 6 April 1892, Charles Ellis Johnson, LDS Church Archives.

Index

INDEX